IRiSHOLOGY

IRISHOLOGY

SLAGGING, JUNIOR C
FOOTBALL, WET RAIN
AND EVERYTHING ELSE
WE LOVE ABOUT
IRELAND

~~~

RONAN MOORE

GILL BOOKS

GiLL BOOKS
HUME AVENUE
PARK WEST
DUBLiN 12
WWW.GiLLBOOKS.iE

Gill Books is an imprint of M.H. Gill & Co.

© Ronan Moore 2015

978 07171 6820 0

Design by Fidelma Slattery
Illustrations by Fuchsia MacAree
Printed by BZ Graf, Poland

This book is typeset in Daft Brush and Gotham.

The paper used in this book comes from the wood pulp of
managed forests. For every tree felled, at least one tree is
planted, thereby renewing natural resources.

A CIP catalogue record for this book is available
from the British Library.

5 4 3

For Frances, whose love and support lights my way.

For family and friends, home and abroad, whom I hold so dear.

Thanks to everyone who helped and to Ger for your advice.

And finally to Deirdre et al for making it happen.

WET RAIN

There are 466 types of rain in Ireland, some 65% of them indigenous to the country. Of all the rains, perhaps the nation's favourite is 'wet rain', commonly associated with a 'soft day'.

This rain, which exists nowhere else on the planet, is somewhere along the spectrum between a mist and a drizzle and is best known for its ability to lull you into believing that you won't need a jacket for the walk down to the pub.

However as soon as you get in the front door, you realise that your jumper is absolutely and utterly soaked and you'll have a chest infection by midnight.

WiLDLY iNAPPROPRiATE SPEED LiMiT SiGNS

Dangerous bends ahead? Accident black spot? Barely enough space for two large vehicles to pass? It doesn't matter, let's make it 100 km/h, it's all good.

In Ireland, applying rational decision-making to road speed markings has never been our forte, leading to some of the most wildly inappropriate speed limit signs in Western Europe. There are countless examples of wide, open stretches of road that you could safely land a plane onto but that are still only signposted for 80 km/h. And for every one of these, you have a 'national route' where no matter how safe or dangerous it may be, only 100 km/h will do!

Of all these roads, and there are many, my favourite must be the Athboy to Delvin road where on one 200-metre stretch, a driver is met first with 'Dangerous Bends', and then immediately reminded that '100 km/h' is still grand, before an 'Accident Black Spot' completes the set.

POTATOES

Baked potatoes, fried potatoes, boiled potatoes, potato cakes, potato skins, chips, crisps, roast potatoes, garlic potatoes, potatoes dauphinoise (for the landed classes).

New potatoes, flowery potatoes, lovely potatoes.

Potatoes: the king and queen of Irish vegetables! So good a million Irish people died for them and another million and half went off to America looking for more.

When I was growing up potatoes were such a staple food we didn't even count them as a vegetable. They were simply a presence in our household, like the television and the picture of the Sacred Virgin.

In the years since, while rice and pasta may have made inroads into the Irish dinner-time, the humble potato remains the nation's favourite. Nutritious, filling and multi-talented, the potato can do almost anything except deal with muggy, wet weather.

LIGA

In Ancient Sparta they had a tradition that if a baby appeared weak at birth, they would leave it out overnight in the elements. If the infant survived the night, it would be taken back in and raised a Spartan so that one day, covered in baby oil, it would do battle for Sparta.

For generations in Ireland we had a similar tradition. Except instead of leaving our babies outside, we gave them Liga.

According to some sources, Liga was the '*ideal supplement to baby's diet*'. However to those of us who remember, it was more than that. It was the marathon of baby foods that your mouth did battle with for hours in order to break it down and get through to those essential vitamins and minerals. Many babies didn't make it but for those of us who did, we grew stronger. And as the adverts used to show, by the time we reached nine months of age, not only had we developed vocal chords strong enough to call Mama and Dada but also to utter that famous battle-cry of baby freedom:

'I WANT MY LIGA!'

TiN WHiSTLES

IT'S A WHiSTLE MADE OF TiN!

Wikipedia lists the tin whistle as a musical instrument. This seems a little flattering as it is probably easier to get a musical note by strangling a small family pet than by blowing into these yokes.

That doesn't stop tens of thousands of Irish children being given them in primary school each year and told to head off to the corner and learn 'Twinkle, Twinkle, Little Star'. I can still remember the noise my tin whistle would make: a disturbance of air waves that I wouldn't hear the like of again until a particularly acute case of gastroenteritis many, many years later.

Of course I realise now that they were never meant to be learnt but were simply an instrument used to test whether children had the patience to be moved on to a proper musical instrument, like the recorder.

BROWN BREAD (AKA SODA BREAD)

Brown bread: slow-releasing, super-delicious and what should always be served with any self-respecting Irish soup.

Our family recipe came from my Mam, whose recipe came from her Mam, whose recipe probably came from her Mam, *ad infinitum*:

- A fistful of wheat meal
- Two fistfuls of flour
- Two teaspoons of bread soda
- One teaspoon of salt
- One teaspoon of baking powder
- And don't forget the ... family secret

Along with sandwiches and soups, one other serving suggestion is to gently drizzle brown sauce over some slices and then fry it along with some butter, promising never to tell your GP about it. For a healthier option, substitute margarine for the butter.

TCP

TCP, aka trichlorophenylmethyliodosalicyl: used by Irish mothers and grandmothers for eons to treat any number of medical illnesses from nettle stings and sore throats to crotch rot and cerebral malaria.

While the last pair of ailments be a stretch, very little can escape a splash of TCP to help make things better. Smelling like a 1980s nursing home, TCP is to the Irish family medicine kit as the cross is to Christianity.

My favourite TCP memory is from when I was 8 years old and in my neighbour's house. While there, the family dog (probably called Toby) bit me through the sleeve of my sister's hand-me-down-but-thankfully-quite-bulky coat. As the dog had pierced the skin, I received a splash of the good old TCP, was told not to scare the dog in future, and sent on my way.

AN GARDA SÍOCHÁNA

If the number of television programmes made about you is anything to go by, then An Garda Síochána get nowhere near the level of respect as a police force as their counterparts do in the United States.

If the Gardaí do not get the level of respect they deserve, this is a pity as something must be said for a law enforcement agency that decides that the best way to police its communities is without the use of guns! They often go out in the worst conditions armed only with an extendable baton and a sandwich from the local Centra to make sure our communities are safe.

Having been originally created as an armed police force, the Provisional Government reversed the decision and reconstituted the force as unarmed. The rationale for this came in the words of the first Commissioner of Police, Michael Staines: *'the Garda Síochána will succeed not by force of arms or numbers, but on their moral authority as servants of the people'*. And for that you have to applaud them.

It's just a pity some of them have trouble pronouncing the word 'vehicle'.

WALL-PAPERED COPYBOOKS

---- First came walls.

---- Then came wall-paper.

---- Then came wall-papered copybooks.

It was an Ireland where the family was sacred, the front room was sacred and school copybooks were sacred, so parents did what they could to protect them. So every summer, when they finished wall-papering the front room, they used the remainder to wall-paper all the school copybooks for the coming year.

We didn't have wall-paper in our house, so instead we used brown paper. This did just as a good a job though it never had any bubbles in it that you could squash down or peel off.

Nowadays things have changed. Some say it is the liberal agenda; others believe it is because you can no longer get your hands on good quality wall-paper. Either way if you look in any school classroom you will see copybooks – geography, history and science – all tragically going uncovered.

TRAD SESSiONS

Your foot starts tapping without any permission given. Then comes the hand. Finally your head starts to nod. A pint of stout is in front of you, your friends beside. It's a full-blown trad session. There will be no leaving the pub any time soon.

There is something genuinely special about traditional Irish music. Played well it doesn't just take the individual but the whole crowd, and brings it off on a meandering journey. This meander reminds me a little of jazz. However while jazz can sometimes resemble a group of men stuck in a room unable to find their way out but who keep playing until they do, trad musicians are already out of the room and off playing their way through life. They don't know how it is going to end but for some reason neither you nor they care. Such is life.

Traditional music makes trad sessions and trad sessions are the original flash mobs – they can begin randomly any-where at any time. The makings of the best trad sessions usually go something along the following lines: a few friends meet up in a pub armed with a fiddle, a guitar, a concertina and a tin whistle. Random people then start to show up who may have no connection whatsoever to the original members, armed with instruments that can range from a bodhrán to a pair of spoons. Numbers continue to grow, both playing and listening, until the place is packed.

The energy of the place continues to grow as the building itself begins to heave and breath to the sounds being played. At some stage a middle-aged man will lose control of himself out the back and shout out something beginning with a 'Y' like '*Yippee!*', '*Yahoo!*' or '*Ya boya!*' Everyone else will turn round and smile, notice the barman is trying to get a pint of Smithwicks out to re-supply the banjo player, hand it across to him and then continue to enjoy.

At the very best sessions the barman will eventually bring things to a close by telling everyone it is in fact now Tuesday, and they are two days late for work.

THE CONFIRMATION

A confirmation is a Christian rite of passage for the purpose of bestowing the Gift of the Holy Spirit. In Ireland there are four essential parts:

1. THE NAME PART: You get to choose a new name! Well, that is the theory. In practice it is a middle, middle name and it isn't really a choice. If it were a choice, half my class would have called themselves Diego and the other half Madonna. Instead you have to choose an Irish saint's name. I plumped for Kevin because I associated him with nature and it scored well in Scrabble.

2. THE WINDFALL PART: Like share dividends, you can expect a small financial pay-out from your relations to help celebrate the occasion. Despite getting just £24 for my communion, I fully expected to break the £50 mark this time around. In the end I got just £27, which, adjusted for inflation, was actually down on my communion take!

3. THE PLEDGE PART:

At this point in the confirmation proceedings you stand up with your class-mates and read out a holy pledge and receive a badge. You aren't entirely sure what the pledge means except that it involves alcohol and you are going to break it the first chance you get.

4. THE RELIGIOUS PART:

Finally there is something about confirming what you first agreed to when you were 4 months old. In effect this means you are now a fully signed-up member of the Catholic Church and that you agree to never support Glasgow Rangers.

SLOW SETS

Thought to have originated during the showband era of the 1960s, slow sets were a 20-minute period of romantic songs that allowed members of the opposite sex to chase each other down and ask the question '*would you like to dance with me?*' For men (for 'men', read 'me'), positive responses usually numbered in the less-than-20% range but all that meant was that if you were prepared to ask at least five different girls, the law of averages meant that at least one would agree (for 'agree', read 'cave').

By the early 1990s slow sets had become an integral part of any disco with two or three 20-minute sets that spanned the musical spectrum with songs from Celine Dion and Bryan Adams to Whitney Houston and Rod Stewart.

When the slow set arrived, where you once had friends, you now only had adversaries as each friend started searching (for 'searching', read 'hunting') for that girl they had spotted earlier beside the cloakroom. I can remember from my own juvenile disco days the sudden panic that would break out once a bit of Chris de Burgh opened up and the lights went dim.

Slow sets only lasted for 20 minutes and if you hadn't found anyone by Wet Wet Wet's 'Love is All Around', then that was it: your chance at gnashing against someone else's teeth was up, at least for another week.

Sadly, slow sets are no longer commonplace around the country, and now join letter-writing, sitting around a radio and being drafted into the army as traditions our children will never fully appreciate.

MAIN STREETS

Nothing characterises a traditional Irish town more than its main street. Not only are they great places to bump into that guy from school you recognise but whose name you can't quite remember, they're also a stretch of road where you can complete all your weekend errands.

While there are no prerequisites as to what constitutes a main street, they usually contain most or all of the following: two pubs; a post office; a hardware store; a clothes shop; a fruit and veg shop advertising Kerr Pinks; another pub; a coffee shop; a bank with someone collecting for a local GAA club outside; a credit union; one more pub; a newsagents; two betting shops (usually at either ends of the street); a pub-cum-shop; and a hair salon called 'A Cut Above', 'Always Hair for You' or 'Curl Up and Dye'.

Another interesting fact is that despite main streets being on average three times as wide as most ordinary urban thoroughfares, they remain traffic black spots as men called Seán or Mícheál or women called Máire or Joan stick the hazards on while they go off to buy stamps.

BLACK PUDDING

I get mixed feelings when I think about pigs. On the one hand they are tasty. On the other hand they are horrid cute. But then on the other hand they are tasty.

One of these days I will stop eating pig. However in the meantime, I'm glad that in Ireland we don't tend to waste any of it when we do eat it. This is where black pudding comes in.

If ever there was a food that should be consumed first before it is explained, black pudding is that food. *'Black pudding: A type of sausage made by cooking dried pigs' blood with a filler until it is thick enough to congeal when cooled.'* Food or punishment?

While it might sound as appetising as 'road-kill a l'orange' there are fewer things as tasty as a bit of warm black pudding, whether it be in a full Irish breakfast or apple salad starter.

RED LEMONADE

≳ Soft drink to the proletariat? ≲

≳ Opiate of the masses? ≲

≳ Health fad? ≲

≳ Lifestyle choice? ≲

≳ Teeth discolourer? ≲

Red lemonade means many different things to many different people. For me it was something my parents would buy me and my siblings while they enjoyed an evening drink on the way home from visiting relatives. While it was a soft drink that had more E's in it than a Manchester rave it was also cheap, even in the glass bottle, and that meant more spare 20p pieces for the pool table.

Red lemonade never managed to make it out of Ireland. Part of this may be attributed to Pan-European Food and Drug Administration's making it an offence to sell the stuff and part of this may have been marketing. I mean, can you imagine red lemonade being pitched on an episode of 'Dragon's Den'?

Pitcher: *'It's a new soft drink to the market called red lemonade.'*
Dragon: *'So it's a drink made of lemons coloured red?'*
Pitcher: *'Yes and no. It is red but there are no lemons.'*
Dragon: *'So what is actually made of?'*
Pitcher: *'I can't say.'*
Dragon: *'What do you mean, you can't say?'*
Pitcher: *'If I tell you they'll kill me.'*
Dragon: *Silence*
Pitcher: *Silence*
Dragon: *Silence*
Pitcher: *Silence*
Dragon: *Silence*
Pitcher: *'It tastes great in whiskey.'*

THE CLADDAGH RING

Nothing says '*my love is up for grabs*' like a Claddagh ring with the heart pointing outwards worn on the right hand. Or is it the left?

Originally produced in the Galway fishing village of Claddagh, the Claddagh ring is usually given to a woman, either by her lover or passed down from her mother. Distinctive in design, its heart, crown and hands are said to represent love, loyalty and friendship.

There was further symbolism attached to it that me and my male friends paid particular attention to while growing up. Depending on how it was worn, you could tell if someone was spoken for or not. For instance:

♥ Worn on the right hand with the point of the heart towards the finger-tips, the wearer is single and may be looking for love.

♥ Worn on the right hand with the point of the heart towards the wrist, the wearer is in a relationship and her heart has been 'captured'.

♥ Worn on the left hand with the point of the heart towards the finger-tips, the wearer is engaged.

♥ Worn on the left hand with the point of the heart towards the wrist, the wearer is married (something you would generally didn't encounter at any of the juvenile discos I was at).

Of course it rarely worked. This was partly due to the fact that most girls didn't really care how they wore the ring, partly due to teenage boys' inability to remember the rules of the ring and partly due to the fact that, bar grabbing the girl's hand, it was very difficult to actually see in soft lighting which way the heart pointed. Thankfully, these days we have Tinder to help ascertain someone's relationship status and the Claddagh ring can go back to just being beautiful.

CRiSPS

Along with our passports, blotchy skin and occasional bad teeth, one other thing that helps identify us as Irish is how we pronounce the word 'crisps'. While this might be a source of amusement in some quarters, it should be a badge of honour for the Irish because when you have crisps of the quality of Tayto and King, you can pronounce crisps however the hell you want. While in the past Tayto and King crisp eaters and their respective habits were as divided as Free Staters and Republicans, nowadays there are only three types of crisp eaters in Ireland:

1.

Those who eat crisps one by one as they look wistfully out a train window

2.

Those who eat crisps by the handful as they count down the final few minutes of a football game

3.

Those who eat crisp sandwiches*

*Crisp sandwiches: an Irish culinary delicacy that involves lazily draping crisps between two slices of white pan, with or without a wisp of butter.

TURF FIRES

It is universally recognised that Irish people love turf fires. Often in the middle of a conversation about something entirely unrelated such as politics or pop music, someone might call out '*Jaysus, there's nothing like a turf fire!*' While the chances of this interjection rise during bouts of cold weather (September through to May), the general response will usually be, '*ah yeh, turf fires are great*' before everyone returns to the topic at hand.

Less universally recognised is the fact that only about 2% of the Irish population has experienced a turf fire outside of the pub. If they had, they would realise that feeding these unproductive heating monsters is a full-time job and that you have to be within two feet of them to genuinely benefit from some warmth, space that you will have to fight half your family, the pet dog, Rover, and Peig for.

But all that aside, Jaysus, there's nothing like a turf fire!

SLAGGiNG

slagging

/'slagɪŋ/

Noun (informal)

1. An insulting and critical attack.

'I knew I would get a slagging for that comment'

(not to be mixed up with mining, steel mills or slag pits)

There are very few countries in the world where you can start off a conversation with a friend you haven't seen in over a decade by calling him a bollix, i.e. *'How are ya, ya old bollix?!'* In fact it doesn't even have to be an old friend, it could be the beginnings of a new friendship. I knew one guy who initiated his first ever conversation with me by calling me a *'brown-nosing bollix who should be ashamed to con-sider himself Irish'* because I was going to cook food for my boss and his wife instead of meeting a fellow immigrant Irishman for a pint. He is now one of my closest friends.

Irish people slag each other in the same way a dog might bark at crows. It just comes natural. To other nationalities it might appear as the gravest of insults but to us, it is a way of establishing bonds of friendships and becoming at ease with a mate.

There are many ways to slag someone:

◆ For men, commenting on their lack of facial or head hair, how tight they are with money, or that they rang their ex-girlfriend at three in the morning (again) are all good ways to start.

◆ For women, commenting on their lack of facial or head hair, how tight they are with money, or that they rang their ex-boyfriend at three in the morning (again) are all good ways to start. Okay, maybe not so much on the hair.

It is important to note that under no circumstances should you mention their mother, their children or that they have put on weight, particularly around the posterior.

THE LOCAL

THE LOCAL IS A PLACE ...

... where you feel welcome and can allow the weight of the world fall off your shoulders in the time it takes your pint to settle.

... where what little sun there might be can stream through the side window as you read the day's paper.

... where some mongrel collie sits happily near his master's feet, content to be in out of the rain.

... where the pool table is in the corner and has just one good pool cue.

... where the hand-dryer in the men's is perpetually out of order and has been since you hit puberty.

... where the barman has known you from when you said you were 18 through to when you actually turned 18 and for the 18 years since.

... where everybody knows your name.

FUNGIE THE DOLPHIN

LOST?
GAY?
MiSUNDERSTOOD?
DEAD?

Since Fungie the bottlenose dolphin turned up in Dingle Harbour back in 1984, there have been more rumours about him than you would expect of an Oscar-nominated child actor. Over the years many a tabloid gossip panel has headlined with this beloved Kerry-based marine animal:

★ 'Fungie is my father, lovechild claims'

★ 'Fungie checked into rehab clinic to recover from sleeping tablets addiction'

★ 'Fungie dead again, found in hotel room'

★ 'Fungie ate my hamster'

Of course most of these have all proved to be groundless and Fungie has continued to entertain the boatloads of tourists who come out to visit him and say hello. Despite his popularity, visible in the bronze statue unveiled in Dingle in his honour, very little is known about Fungie. For all we know, he could be a dolphin version of Skippy the bush kangaroo trying to alert us to the plight of little Timmy trapped down the mine-shaft or desperately telling us to leave the planet before it is too late. Unfortunately we don't understand his funny little clicking sounds so we must make do with taking cute photographs of him.

While bottlenose dolphins have a life-span of approximately 25 years, Fungie, believed to have been born in the 1970s, is still rocking well into his forties and, in the words of one local tourist agent, is expected to keep rocking for the next 40 years too.

THE DINGLE ENQUIRER

FUNGIE: FOR PRESIDENT?

JUNiOR C FOOTBALL

It is Sunday morning, cold and wet, and you have been tasked with marking a man twice your age, triple your size and half your speed. The first ball comes in and as you turn, he sucker-punches you in the stomach, collects the knock-down and puts it over the bar. He will move a distance of 187 yards the entire match, score 1–4 and will drink four pints of Guinness by evening. It can only be Junior C football.

Junior C football: where juvenile boys get their first taste of senior football and where senior, senior footballers come to die. It is not a pretty sight and neither is the dressing-room afterwards. The only thing worse than the sight of a Junior C football dressing-room is the smell of it, a heady mixture of last night's Smithwicks, Deep Heat and Lynx deodorant.

While Junior C football might not sound the most inviting, there is something warm and welcoming about it. It is a place where the young footballer and the retiring one, separated by almost two decades, as well as a handful of 'cat' footballers who can't make the second team, sit side by side and converse like father and son. Except with a hell of lot more swearing.

It is a place where as a young lad, when the sucker-punches get too much, you can always count on your elder corner-back counterpart to come in and thump 'your man', unleashing a mini schmozzle and two red cards. It is a band of brothers who haven't cleaned their boots since the last match and have chosen to answer the call of the manager all because of the parish and the fact that, well, sure what else would they be doing after mass on a Sunday?

THE '90S WEATHER FORECAST

'*Aaaaaaaaaand hello there.*' Gerry Fleming. The weatherman's weatherman and a sex symbol before Ireland knew what sex symbols were. Of course he was neither. He was just a lovely fella from Wexford who was actually a meteorologist. And we loved him.

Long before global warming, climate change and Twitter, there were only two constants in Irish weather: rain and Gerald 'Gerry' Fleming's wink. At the beginning of each broadcast, he would start with an elongated '*Aaaaaaaaaand hello there*'.

Such was the nation's trust in Gerry that he could have summarised with, '*So that's scattered showers and a plague of locusts spreading nationwide from the west followed by the Four Horseman of the Apocalypse before finally brightening up later on in the evening with a resurrection of the dead. That's it from me now, bye, bye.*' and Gerry's wink of the eye at the end would put the nation at ease.

SEAN-NÓS SiNGiNG

Sean-nós (Irish for 'old style') singing is a highly ornamented style of unaccompanied traditional Irish singing. Basically it's when everyone gets told to shut up in a pub because a woman you have never seen before, in fact probably no one has ever seen before, walks in and starts to sing during the break of a trad session.

You can't understand a word she is saying because you got a D2 in your Ordinary Level Leaving Cert Irish. However you know it's probably about someone who died, who people grieved for, or for an affection that was never met, or a love that was lost. And you avoid eye-contact with your mates because you start to well up inside, but that's okay because they're avoiding eye-contact with you because they're getting all misty-eyed too.

And then she finishes and leaves forever, taking someone's heart with her, to the grave probably, and he's already dead but probably just doesn't know it yet. And you turn back to your friends and you're like, '*Jaysus!*', and you take a drink to compose yourself and no one will ever see the woman again.

CATTLE-GRiDS

Falling into the category of 'stuff city people have never seen', cattle-grids are metal grilles that formed the first line of defence for rural dwellings long before anyone had even heard of 'Eircom Phone Watch'. As alien to town-folk as a game of kerbs is to those of rural Ireland, the cattle-grid's job is to mind against the unwanted presence of one of the most malevolent forces on the country road: the lost cow.

Everyone from the country knows what a stray cow can do to a manicured lawn, and cattle grids meet this danger head-on, keeping rural gardens bovine-free. An added bonus is that cattle-grids also help stave off the unwanted attention of:

- High-heeled Paris and London Fashion week models
- Long John Silver
- Zombies
- Stilt-walkers
- James A. Roumeliotis
- Unicorns

FAiRY FORTS

A fairy fort is an entrance to the other world where fairies live. Obviously. You will know them by their circular mound, with or without an old hawthorn tree on top. You'll also know them by the septic toe (at the very least) you will get if you try to blast them.

You don't mess with fairy forts. As any a good farmer will tell you, the consequences of messing with these mystical, mythical mounds are many. Indeed, there are several stories of people your neighbour's granddad knows who bulldozed a fairy fort and then died in their sleep 30 years later!

ICE-CREAM VANS

Put a bunch of children together and you will get an ice-cream van. Put a bunch of children together in a housing estate, like the one I grew up in, and you will get two. Add weather above 15°C and you've got an ice-cream van epidemic.

A parent's nightmare, a child's dream, there is nothing quite like the feeling of tearing into the kitchen in search of your Mam when you hear the unmistakable sound of the ice-cream van. A mixture of panic and exhilaration sets in as children, up until then playing tig, Tip the Can or football with jumpers for goalposts, detonate off the street and into their homes looking for an adult, any adult, to get money for a 99 and a flake.

The FBI couldn't hunt down an escaped prisoner any quicker than children finding parents hiding behind couches, curtains and in the hot press. Through tantrums and tears, hard cash is extracted as the kids explode back into the streets to catch Mr Whippy and its owner, who always has a moustache, always.

While other countries have ice-cream vans, what really sets Ireland's apart is the fact that ours operate under a law of their own. They can play their 'Teddy Bears' Picnic' for as long as they want. They can stop at the end of the road for as long as they like. And they don't need to wait until the temperature hits 15°C before they come out. Anytime, any-where, any weather. Just as long as there's children.

ROCK SHANDY

The soft drink of the middle classes. Some of us know where we were the day JFK was shot or when the Twin Towers came down. Some of us also remember the day when an out-of-town kid arrived into the bar where we played pool as our Dads drank Smithwicks and ordered a rock shandy.

Half Club Lemon, half Club Orange, the rock shandy was so upmarket that not only did it come close to costing the same as a pint of the black stuff, the barman would also throw in a slice of orange!

Some of us passed it off as a fad, a decadence, a Babylonian excess that was as much responsible for hole in the ozone layer as the punctured fridge dumped at the end of your uncle's boreen. However for those of us who made the mistake of tasting it, we were hooked, and red lemonade would never sparkle as red ever again.

THE LENT BOX

'You know, there are children in Africa starving.' And with this parental remark many a 1980s child would look down at the yellowy orange mush on the side of their plate and feel guilty for not eating this muck. Of course it wasn't muck, it was a type of root vegetable; but for any 9-year-old worth their salt, it was muck.

The main evidence for the starving children in Africa was the old Lent boxes that appeared during every Lenten period into which you would throw in a few coppers every time you thought of a sin – which was a lot in old Catholic Ireland.

Thankfully things have moved on and Lent boxes nowadays are much more positive in their appearance and give a much stronger message of how the few cents that you drop in will help the smiling faces that now adorn them attain justice and equity.

Unfortunately 9-year-olds still think yellowy orange root vegetables are muck.

THE SHAMROCK

Legend has it that, keen to win over local Irish leaders to Christianity, St Patrick searched desperately for something to help him to explain its central tenets. Unable to get reception on his smartphone to access Wikipedia, St Patrick had to think on his feet. However with only nettles, dock leaves and dandelions around him, things were looking pretty grim – until he spotted the trusty shamrock.

It proved to be a real stroke of luck: the shamrock, already well regarded as a symbol in pre-Christian Ireland, was the perfect illustration for the Holy Trinity. Pointing to its three leaves, he spoke about how these represented the Father, Son and the Holy Spirit and just as the leaves were different but part of the same plant, so too were the parts of the Holy Trinity different but also the same.

It worked. Soon Irish people started to convert to Christianity. And that is the origin of how the shamrock became a symbol of Ireland and why a bowl of the mossy stuff has been handed to slightly bewildered-looking US presidents every St Patrick's Day for the last 60 years.

SHIFTING

The French usually refer to it as '*embrasser*'; the Spanish say '*besos*' and the Germans use '*küssen*'. All romantic-sounding terms for that passionate practice otherwise known as kissing. Except in Ireland where we call it '*shifting*'.

Oh yes, Don Juan O'Neill. I mean, where else would you make the sweet sense of lips touching, tongues tingling, mouths closing sound like moving furniture? I mean, really, '*shifting*'?!

Yet every weekend tens of thousands of young people go out in search of '*the shift*'. And then, come Monday morning, reports hit the school yard, college campus or workplace of Michael shifting Mary, Niamh shifting Noel, and Fergal shifting Fiona. To an uninformed passer-by it might sound like there was a hell of a lot of office movement going on over the weekend. In truth it was just young Irish love taking place, with perhaps a little too much saliva.

BATCH BREAD

Long before gluten was invented, bread was the kingpin and staple component of the Irish weekday lunch. And amongst this bread, one type reigned supreme: the batch loaf. While it was true that batch bread couldn't bend without breaking, making it impossible to carry a sandwich around in your pocket, batch had character. The bakers knew this and as a result it was rightfully more expensive than its cousin, the sliced pan. Another interesting fact about batch was that, in much the same way as families were divided between Fianna Fáil and Fine Gael, houses were equally divided between those that fought over the heel of the batch loaf and those who were happy to watch it go stale at the back of the bread bin.

Unfortunately though, with EU accession and the free movement of bread, batch's popularity soon began to wane. Foreign breads like baguettes, paninis and ciabattas started to move in, taking lunch jobs as they were prepared to work for less, thus making the sight of the occasional top of a batch slice hanging awkwardly out of a toaster a very rare thing indeed nowadays.

FiG ROLLS

Ask many an Irish person and they will say Fig Rolls are quintessentially Irish. This is a little strange considering:

> Only 0.09% of Irish people even known what a fig is.

> Only 0.005% of Irish people have ever seen an actual fig.

> The fact that Fig Rolls as a biscuit actually date back to Ancient Egypt.

Still it could be worse — we could be laying claim to the pyramids. Of course the real reason Fig Rolls are quintessentially Irish is because back in mid-1980s Ireland, the advertising department of Jacob's Biscuits asked the question, '*how do Jacob's get the figs into the Fig Rolls?*' And so it began. Fig Rolls took on legendary status and became every bit a mystery to 1980s Ireland as the Mary Celeste, Shergar and the Third Secret of Fatima.

ST PATRICK'S DAY PARADES

St Patrick's Day Parades are as much part of Ireland's national holiday as the Club Championships, terrible weather and the occasional bout of inebriation. While Dublin and the major towns and cities often put on spectacular floats to wow spectators, at the coalface in local towns and villages across the country things are a lot more rustic.

The average St Patrick Day Parade contains the following:

- 4 old tractors

- A fire-brigade that occasionally sounds its siren, which may be for the children or may be because they genuinely want to get to a house-fire

- Hailstones

- 6 juvenile sports teams with children who can no longer feel their ears

- A delay

- At least one car that drove into the parade by the mistake, whose occupants look mortified as they drive in front of the U-14 football team

- A marching band, usually from the US, who thought they were coming to a much larger town

- A burst of sunshine

- 5 more old tractors

- A waste disposal company carrying a bale of rubbish, advertising a waste disposal company

- Showers

- Another delay

- Two dozen transit vans with balloons tied to their rear-view mirrors, or as many it takes to cover the costs of the parade

- A man leading a sheep

- A local dance troupe with an 11-year-old who keeps dropping her baton on the ground but that's okay as she is the child of proud parents somewhere

- Wind

- A vintage car driven by someone who looks familiar but who you just don't know the name of

- More delays

- A céilí band playing music on the back of an old tractor

- Either a re-enactment of something from our past or a gangland turf war involving swords

- 3 more old tractors

And at the end of it, families return home with children either enamoured with old tractors or wanting to learn the baton and parents saying comments like '*sure last year was shite as well*'. Secretly though, we all love it.

'ONE MORE'

It is not entirely sure where the Irish custom of *'one more'* comes from but it is deeply engrained in Irish culture.

Where this practice is most prominent is in the public house when having come down for just one drink to watch the match, to say hello to some friends, or to unwind after a week's work, someone throws up the idea of 'one more'. This can be expressed in a number of ways: *'one more for the road'*, *'ara, one more won't kill you'* or the profoundly polite *'sure, go on and have one more, ya bollix, sure haven't I gone already and bought it for you!'*

At this stage the chances of you leaving the bar have reduced dramatically and you have as much chance of getting home sober as Ireland does to escape rain during the month of April. Soon one more turns into one more before the match starts, which then becomes one more while we watch the match and one more before we leave before finally one more now that we are in the night-club.

Next thing you know you haven't slept all night and are at a Ryanair counter with your old mate Touhy enquiring about the prices of an air fare to Edinburgh.*

However 'one more' is not just reserved to the consumption of alcohol. Other Irish contexts where you might come across this maxim include:

- *'Ara, sure one more cup of tea won't do you any harm'* – popular suggestion by your aunt

- *'Ara, sure one more Mikado won't kill me'* – popular response to your aunt

- *'Ara, sure one more mortgage won't make a difference'* – popular idea during the Celtic Tiger

*€264 was the price of a one-way ticket.

IRISH MOTHERS

SAMPLE CHARACTERISTICS OF AN IRISH MOTHER:

★ Her son is the best.

★ Shrapnel wounds are more preferable to her scowl.

★ Only she knows where the good china is.

★ When a visitor arrives she can have the kettle boiled, the tea brewed, a few sandwiches made and the Mikado biscuits out in less than 43 seconds.

★ Bringing over a guest without giving prior notice to clean up is a crime akin to infanticide in her eyes.

★ That said, with notice she doesn't mind if you do bring a couple of friends back – but only a few, mind.

★ She always knows where the cat is.

★ She is fascinated by her daughter's hair and may take a brush to it if given any opportunity.

★ If she doesn't approve of your girlfriend, you're screwed.

★ Her arch enemy is a mysterious figure only known as 'the Draught'.

★ She has sole ownership of the word 'gallivanting'.

★ Nobody cooks better than her and sure the sausages are already made so you may as well have one.

★ Whenever a son or daughter is leaving the house, she is obliged under law to ask *'Are you bringing a coat with you?'*

OTHER FAVOURITE QUESTIONS INCLUDE:

— *'Do you want tea?'*

— *'When are you going to settle down and get married?'*

— *'Are you messing?'*

— *'Didn't I tell you if you continued messing that would happen?'*

— *'Are you going to tidy up that before your father gets home?'*

— *'Are you getting up today?'*

— *'Would you not eat something before heading out?'*

— *'Do you want tea before you go?'*

— *'Are you sure you're alright?'*

— *'You're sure, you're sure?'*

We love them deeply.

LOCAL LEGENDS

Every community has them. They are the man who delivered oil; the army private; the family doctor; the guy up in college in Dublin; the miner; the sport's shop proprietor; the dairy farmer; the primary-school teacher. You can be guaranteed there is at least one who works for the bank. They are the men and women from the local community who by day seem almost ordinary but on summer Sundays, representing their community and county, they line out for All-Ireland Championship football, hurling or camogie in front of tens of thousands of screaming fans.

In my little village it was Mick Lyons. He was tough as nails. I knew he was tough as nails because his surname was Lyons, he was huge and I swear I once saw him cycle a bicycle with one hand holding a plank of wood and the other arm in plaster! Such was his ferocity on the field a team-mate once said that parents should '*keep a photograph of Mick Lyons on the mantle-piece to keep children away from the fire*'. I can't remember him without a smile though, on those few occasions I remember seeing him in the village or when visiting our school. He was the full-back for our county team and our local legend.

RYANAiR

- If you make a mistake with your booking, they make you pay.

- If you spell your name wrong on your boarding card, they make you pay.

- If you don't have a boarding card, they make you pay.

- If your bag is a shoelace overweight, they make you pay.

- If your bag is an uneaten apple away from fitting, they make you pay.

- If you want to ring them to find out why your plane landed almost a country away from it scheduled destination, they make you pay.

- If you complain, they make you pay.

- If you try to change flights, they make you pay.

- If you do anything other than sit down and shut up, they make you pay.

We like to get angry about Ryanair and much of the time it is with proper reason. However we have quickly forgotten what life was like before Ryanair was born in Ireland.

We were an island nation with only one airline. It was an airline that only those who owned second cars, holiday homes or knew what olives tasted like (a very select few in the 1980s) could fly with. And due to this the ferry to England was the height of many families' continental aspirations.

Into this came Ryanair and their man Michael O'Leary. Using a new-fangled system called the internet he coined the term 'low-cost airlines', democratised air travel and showed the world that there really was no limit to the amount of public complaints a company could get in a day!

SPORTS DAYS

No longer as common as they once were, perhaps due to the growth of insurance claims against them, community sports days used to be a mainstay of an Irish village summer.

For one July day the local GAA field would be taken over by a whole manner of activities that seemed to have little or no connection with actual sport. It was almost always sunny, almost always a little chaotic and almost always great fun. The timetable for an Irish sports day used to run something like this:

10.00AM: OFFICIAL START
Actual start usually happens an hour later.

11.00AM: SKIP-A-THON
Beginning at the far corner of the field this 15-minute event would continue right until the end of the evening, with the winner usually a 13-year-old girl in a time of 6 hours 37 minutes.

11.10AM: SACK RACE

Of course rarely did anyone ever use sacks. Instead plastic cattle-feed bags were employed, irrespective of whether you had cattle or not. The winner would be any person who actually had a proper sack, with the rest cannoning into the ground a few metres from the finish line.

11.20AM: EGG-AND-SPOON RACE

Once again the name was a bit of a misnomer as no Irish mother worth her salt would allow any eggs leave the house. Instead everyone lined up with a giant tablespoon and a potato, with the canny ones sticking a dirty thumb-nail into the skin to help with balance.

11.30AM: WHEEL-BARROW RACE

A sack race without sacks, an egg-and-spoon race without eggs and a wheel-barrow race where instead of a wheel-barrow you used a person. Usually over-zealous drivers would ensure that at least one or two 'wheel-barrows' ended with bloody noses as their arms buckled under their drivers' speed and ambition.

11.40AM: THREE-LEGGED-RACE

A race that would see the destruction of half a dozen fathers' ties.

11.50AM: TUG-O-WAR

This was a big hit with the men-folk who, having done absolute no training, would divide themselves by the local bar they drank in and anchor whoever propped up the bar most Friday nights at the end of the line. If they were lucky, the anchor would have no football boots on, slip and an easy victory would be had. If they were unlucky, the battle would go on for 15 minutes until the whole half-back line of the local Junior B hurling team had pulled their hernias.

12.10PM: MOTHERS' RACE

If the tug-o-war was tough, the mothers' race was downright nasty. Despite only taking part due to the encouragement of sons, daughters and husbands (most of whom were now holding their groins), once mothers lined up the gloves came off. Add the slightest traces of mud and things got positively rude. Never a great memory for anyone present.

12.20PM: HURDLES

In case enough carnage hadn't been done, a set of old hurdles were taken out that would lead to at least one child chipping a front tooth.

12.30PM: SLOW-BICYCLE RACE

This final race never proved a hit, generally due to no one really understanding the rules of it and the fact it was shit.

12.40–3.00PM: 'FIELD' EVENTS

At this stage of proceedings, the track events closed and the 'field' events got going. These were often run by outsiders and were usually stacked against the participants. Events involved spinning a wheel, flicking a coin, rolling a coin, guessing something in a jar or on a trailer, shooting caps, tossing a ring and then losing. It was great fun and cost our families a small fortune.

3.00PM: BOUNCY BABY COMPETITION

At this time the tannoy system would finally start working, announce the winner of the bouncy baby competition before going back on the blink as it stated that either a '*law society*' or a '*lost child*' had been found wandering near the far football goals.

3.30PM: SOMETHING INVOLVING ANIMALS

The climax of the day would then take pace with something wildly inappropriate involving farm animals, perhaps best characterised by the notorious Castletown Donkey Derby of 1994.

4.00PM: END

After this, with half the family in need of plasters, proceedings would start to wind down for all concerned, except those whose 13-year-old daughters were still skipping and would continue to do so for the next hour.

TALKiNG ABOUT
THE WEATHER

Extract from my proposed new book *101 ways to
begin a conversation in Ireland*:

YOU BEGiN WiTH:
'How are ya?'

WE WiLL RESPOND WiTH:
'Grand.'
'Not a bother.'
'The finest.'

YOU THEN RETORT WiTH ANY ONE OF THE FOLLOWiNG:
'Great weather we're having.'
'Shite weather we're having.'
'Fine weather we're having.'
'Terrible weather we're having.'
'Some weather we're having.'
'Weather we're having.'

In Ireland the weather dominates conversation in the same way words might elsewhere. In order to begin any sort of dialogue, it is almost mandatory to first spend a couple of minutes talking about the current conditions outside.

Up until only recently it was not uncommon to overhear judges beginning murder trials, cardiologists initiating heart transplants and boxers commencing heavyweight bouts pass their first few minutes by giving their opinion on whether it was going to turn to rain later, with the respective defendant/patient/opponent.

While it is unlikely nowadays that two people will fall out if they don't first commence by complaining about the heat (if we are three days without rain) or about the wet (if we are three hours into a shower), it is only when strangers have conversed about the weather that either party will be truly at ease with one other.

MIDDLE POLITICS

If the entire political spectrum were a football field with the far left in one goal and the far right in the other, the width of Ireland's political spectrum would see us not leave the centre circle.

Voting preferences are generally not based on political philosophies but on:

~ Where you were born.

~ Whether your great-great-grandfather was a fan of the Big Fella, Dev or drove a tram.

~ Whether their candidate played football for the county.

And while this is as ridiculously infuriating as it is entirely uninspiring, something can be said for a politics where the far left and the far right never seem to have gotten a foothold and where real political intolerance, hatred and vitriol are noticeable only through their absence.

HEALERS

⚡ Problem with the back? Go to a healer.

⚡ Allergy to any form of synthetic cloth? Go to a healer.

⚡ A wart on the back of your elbow? Go to a healer.

⚡ Migraines every time you sneeze? Go to a healer.

⚡ Wife about to leave you because of your snoring?
   Go to a healer.

⚡ Mild cardiac arrest? Go to a healer.

⚡ Ebola? Go to a healer.

In Ireland when modern medicine fails there is still one more line of defence that you can turn to: the healer. In every community there is one, or someone who knows one, or failing that someone who knows someone who knows one. Often the seventh son of a seventh son, the healer's role is to give you hope when there is none and to fix that problem – even if the wife is leaving you not because of your snoring but because of your chronic gambling problems.

SCHOOL RETREATS

Part and parcel of the Irish secondary school experience is the annual retreats that class groups are invited to go on. They are a time when pupils of all persuasions (though it helps if you are Catholic) go somewhere down the country, take time out from their busy school schedule and reflect on where life is taking them. Not always easy if you are only 13 and have yet to start shaving.

They are also a time when students get a day off school, make new friends and as long as they don't moon out the back bus window, block the toilets with loo roll or riot immediately after 'silent time', might even get to stop at the shop on the way home.

BOSCO

♪ 'Nananananana-nananananana-nananananana' ♪

While sticking your hand up the ass of a puppet may have had a long tradition stretching back to Punch and Judy and the Muppets, it wasn't until Bosco that puppetry really took off in Ireland.

It must have been an interesting sell to the Irish national television broadcaster RTÉ: a red-haired, genderless 5-year-old puppet with bright red cheeks and a squeaky voice surely must have met with some uncertainty.

But whether it was down to real vision on RTÉ's part or the fact that their only significant financial outlay was going to go on a brightly painted wooden box called the 'bosca' where Bosco lived, it worked and young children loved it. To help Bosco with the heavy lifting, Bosco was joined by two adult presenters, my favourites being Gráinne and Frank.

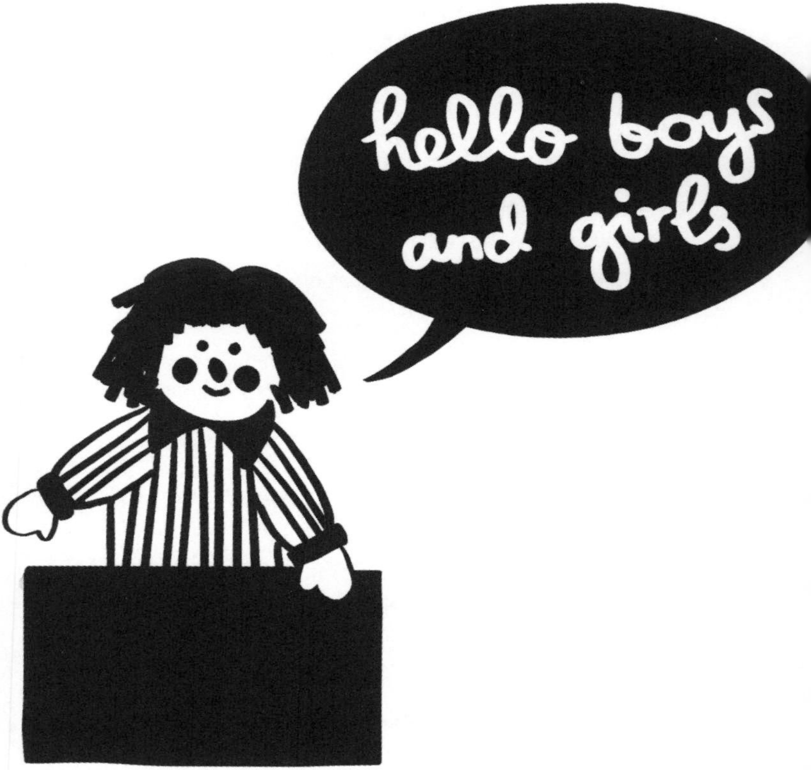
hello boys
and girls

As the years progressed Bosco continued in popularity with the young and started to develop cult status amongst its adult early followers. Rumours started to flourish that the male presenters were on an early-release programme from Mountjoy Prison and Gráinne wasn't even a Catholic. Questions were even asked whether Frank's 'Magic Door' was a gateway drug to more illicit substances.

Of course such stories were all groundless, except maybe for the 'Magic Door', and Bosco remained a firm favourite. While his TV series finally came to a halt in 1987, it was repeated throughout the 1990s, when another generation would hear his welcoming phrase, *'Hello boys and girls'*.

Bosco is still alive and well and, having being acquitted at the Moriarty Tribunal for planning irregularities, he or she currently enjoys a successful theatre career spending his or her time between a 'bosca' in Ireland and one in Spain.

THE ROUNDS SYSTEM

If someone claims to be Irish and you are unsure, two possible ways to find out if they are telling the truth are to:

A: ASK THEM TO EXPLAIN THE ROUNDS SYSTEM

or

B: ASK TO SEE THEIR PASSPORT.

If, with option A, they have no idea what you are talking about, then you know immediately that they have never even been to the island of Ireland. However if they are still rabbiting on after 10 minutes, explaining to you the varying connotations of the rounds system, then you can be pretty safe that they are indeed from home.

At its simplest the rounds system is a technique devised by the Irish to buy drinks in a pub that cannot be explained to anyone, whether that be outsiders or ourselves. The rounds system is so complex that it makes the rules of golf appear like a watered-down version of noughts and crosses. For Irish people though, it is like being born with an innate understanding of quantum physics, except we won't ever win the Nobel Prize for it.

The best general guidance I have yet come across for visitors is:

1.

Buy as many rounds as you're a part of
and the last round before you leave.

2.

Drink with one group at a time.

3.

Don't complain or make mention of money.

While the Irish regularly forgive all but the scabbiest visitors when they mess up the rounds system, they heap praise on those who execute it correctly – so much so that when visiting US President Barack Obama correctly executed buying a round on his visit to Moneygall, County Offaly, some political pundits suggested that this momentum-maker eventually culminated in him winning a second term in office.

FLAT 7UP

It is important to first clarify that Flat 7Up is entirely different to 7Up. 7Up is a brand of lemon-lime-flavoured, non-caffeinated soft drink. Flat 7Up on the other hand is a brand of lemon-lime-flavoured, non-caffeinated soft drink with the bubbles taken out for medicinal purposes.

While one can be reasonably sure that this therapeutic practice did not have its origins in the Famine, the treatment of sick children with Flat 7Up has certainly been on the go for decades. Whether it is an upset stomach or a slight bout of the runs, Irish mothers know best that Flat 7Up is the answer.

First, pour a glass of 7Up (preferably left over from last Christmas). Then, while making a phone-call to the school to explain your sick child's absence, stir the glass with your free hand. By the time you have have finished the call with the secretary that runs into a chat about 'you know who' carrying on with 'herself', the 7Up will be flat and ready to be administered. Always serve with a spoon and the Open University on BBC2 on in the background so the day is not a complete educational write-off.

If conditions worsen, boil the 7Up.

BOiLED EVERYTHiNG

When it comes to cooking, Ireland has never been at the forefront of *haute cuisine*. In the past, we tended to have a direct approach to preparing food: we boiled it.

Potato: boil it

Cabbage: boil it

Cauliflower: boil it

Beetroot: boil it

Egg: boil it

Ham: boil it

Soup: boil it

A sock: boil it

Fish: boil it

Loaf of bread: boil it

Cheese: boil it

Coquilles Saint-Jacques: boil it

It was almost as if we had a primeval instinct for self-preservation that meant as soon as food was harvested, picked or slaughtered, we had to boil it or it would go off.

Then some time a hundred years after the Great Famine, a woman appeared to us from inside a box, which we would later learn to call a television, and told us we no longer needed to boil everything. We could also grill it, fry it, toast it or even flambé it.

Still, as even the most adapted emigrant will tell you, there is something in us, a dirty secret, that every so often looks at a restaurant menu and wishes for something boiled.

KERBS

For half the children of Ireland, who are not from the town, 'kerbs' will mean very little. For the other half (particularly those who grew up before the dawn of the PlayStation and Xbox), kerbs needs little introduction.

Kerbs is the bread and butter of street games. It is the first game you play while you wait for the rest of your mates to turn up for a World Cup/British Bulldog/Tip the Can bonanza. It is also the final game you play with your siblings as the sun sets and you try to squeeze out the last of long summer evenings before your mother calls you in.

It is a classic with the simplest of ingredients and rules.

INGREDIENTS:

- Two kids

- One football (preferably a plastic one costing no more than €5 with a sticker on it saying 'Champion' or 'United')

- Two adjacent kerbs

RULES OF THE GAME:

- Score 100 points to win.

- Take turns throwing ball across to opposite kerb.

- Score 10 points by hitting the opposite kerb at an angle so the ball ricochets back towards you.

- If successful, continue with bonus throws from the middle of the street until you miss. 5 points scored for each successful bonus throw.

These are the basic rules, though of course the scoring and the tenets of the game vary from town to town and estate to estate, with each place adding something different to it. When I was a kid, there was one estate up the town where bonus points were accrued when the ball was successfully thrown over a passing car, while in others extra points came from the type of throw used. On my home turf our speciality was a 20-point bonus if a player managed to strike their opponent (preferably with the ball) as they raced back to the safety of their own kerb after an unsuccessful bonus throw.

Unfortunately the popularity of kerbs has diminished over the years. Part of this reason stems from the fact that it has never been fully recognised as an official GAA sport while part is due to its failed bids to gain admission into the Summer Olympics.

GIVING DIRECTIONS

When it comes to giving directions, the Irish can be as to the point as an elephant's arse. We treat the giving of directions as a murder mystery. We only reveal the way at the very end. Up until then, every road is a suspect, each avenue a possibility. Only when all itineraries are mentioned do we reveal who the murderer is: '*Take the third street on your right and then left after the petrol station, across the humpback bridge and past Colonel Mustard with the candlestick in the Dining Room.*'

THE TYPICAL COURSE OF DIRECTION DIALOGUE:

Driver seeking help: '*Excuse me, sorry, would you know how to get to the Gaelic pitch?*'

Local: '*No problem. If you keep going straight and go past the Lidl and the Aldi, you'll come up to a junction with O'Donoghue's on the corner. If you turn left there, it will bring out Cloncannon direction. You won't want to go out that way.*

'Now, if you go straight ahead instead past the Snug up towards the square past Lawless's Hardware, you'll go out towards Tullamore. And then if you keep going past the Long Bar, Byrne's and the Spar, you'll have gone too far. What you need to then is to turn round and come back into town.

'Now when you get back to the Bank of Ireland, sure you'll have to turn left and you'll find it out that way.

'All right now, best of luck.'

And if you think that sounds clichéd, well then you've never been to Edenderry.

THE BODHRÁN

If musical instruments were metaphors, then the bodhrán would be a cross between a stampede of horses and the human heart.

That is of course when it falls into the hands of an artist. When it falls into the hands of anyone else, it just becomes a nice accompaniment to an Irish football match in much the same way as an inflatable Fyffes banana.

The bodhrán truly is a beautiful instrument and is perhaps the number one reason why goats are happy to pass onto the next world, safe in their knowledge that their hide will soon be making music. When played well, the bodhrán seeps into your skin, emanating out through your feet like few other Irish instruments can and often forms the perfect accompaniment to a trad session.

And such is its power that, while no documented evidence exists, I have heard cases where people have suffered cardiac arrests but have had their hearts sustained for minutes by the beat of a bodhrán until emergency services are safely on the scene.

IRISH WAKES

There is nothing like celebrating life than celebrating the life of someone who has just died. And an Irish wake is just the job for that.

For the uninitiated, a wake is where the loved one (usually dead) is laid out at home and everyone comes to wish them well as they pass from this world to the next. If the person has had a long innings then these events can become one hell of a send-off.

If you have never been to a wake, a few simple instructions should suffice:

~ While there is no clear hierarchy at a wake, generally it goes from immediate family, close friends, extended family, neighbours who bring plates of sandwiches covered with tin-foil, neighbours who don't bring plates, and then you.

~ When you arrive, look to shake hands with someone from the immediate family whose turn it is to look solemn at the doorway. Look sad and tell them that you are *'sorry for their trouble'*.

~ They will then point you to a book that you sign and the front room where the body can be 'viewed'. This book serves as both an attendance list and also as a permission slip to eat sandwiches, soup and a drop of whiskey. Go to the front room first. The tea can wait.

~ Do not worry if children are running around and under the coffin. They will be the sons, daughters and relevant cousins of the immediate family and have probably already eaten their body-weight in biscuits.

~ Walk up to the body and nod solemnly. Say a prayer if you like or something positively nostalgic to the person beside you irrespective of whether you know them. Feel free to touch them on the head (the corpse that is, not the person you've just started talking to).

~ Once these formalities are over with, be prepared to spend anywhere between 10 minutes and several hours being served biscuits, sandwiches, soup and tea.

~ Under no circumstances go looking for an alcoholic drink; it will come to you in due process.

~ Under no circumstances fix the clocks if they are stopped, turn around the mirrors if they are facing the wall or pull the curtain where the body is being viewed.

~ If a priest arrives unexpectedly, follow suit with everyone present. If they stand, you stand. If they stop laughing, you stop laughing. If they hide their poitín, you hide your poitín. Once the priest says a prayer and gets his own glass of poitín, then normalities can resume.

~ Under no circumstances put down your half-pint of porter on the casket, even if it is to free up a hand to take another ham and cheese sandwich.

~ Finally, if you end up in the inner circle supping whiskey at half three in the morning with three men in the front room, be honoured and also prepared to listen to predictions about the local county championships and cattle prices. If you are not a farmer, don't try and offer your opinion on the latter.

FINDING SOMEONE IN COMMON

Ireland is a small place. And because of this, almost everyone is one degree of separation from each other. That is why when two Irish people meet the first thing they will tend to do is try to find out at least one person they both know. Until they find that person, they are pathologically unable to trust each other and the world temporarily goes out of kilter.

While the conversation could take place at a bus stop in Drimnagh, a beach-side hut in the tropics, or in front of firing squad, the line of questioning tends to remain the same:

Irish Person 1: '*Where are you from?*'
Irish Person 2: '*Trim.*'
IP1: '*Do you know Patrick Murphy?*'
IP2: '*I don't think so. Does he play football?*'
IP1: '*No. He used to live in Navan.*'

IP2: *'No, I wouldn't know many over that side.'*

IP1: *'Where did you go to college?'*

IP2: *'Galway.'*

IP1: *'What years were you there?'*

IP2: *'1996 to 1999.'*

IP1: *'I started in 2000.'*

IP2: *'I moved back in 2001.'*

IP1: *'What did you do?'*

IP2: *'I worked with O'Malley's.'*

IP1: *'No way, did you know of a brick-layer called Maurice?'*

IP2: *'Was he from Kinvara?'*

IP1: *'Yes.'*

IP2: *'Yeh, I used to shovel cement for him.'*

IP1: *'No way! Sure he's my uncle! Here, let me buy you a pint.'*

And with that, the seeds of a life-long friendship are formed and the world begins to spin back on its axis.

THE CRAIC

The 'craic' is a rich, hold-all term that may be used for fun, banter, entertainment, gossip, scandal, news and/or conversation. The term itself comes from the English word 'crack' meaning the same. However, possibly because someone in Ireland thought the English weren't using it properly, it was brought over to Ireland, had its spelling changed and was welcomed into Irish culture. It can be sometimes difficult for tourists and the US Drug Enforcement Agency to understand the various meanings of the term 'craic'. To help newcomers along, below is a brief guide to the term:

◆ *Any craic?* – Have you any news?

◆ *What's the craic?* – How are you doing?

◆ *That was some craic!* – That was most entertaining and I thoroughly enjoyed myself.

◆ *Did you hear the craic?* – Have you heard who's pregnant?

◆ *We were just having a bit of craic.* – I don't know how little Paddy broke his right arm or his pelvis; we were just trying to have a bit of fun.

◆ *Sure it might be a bit of craic!* – It will probably be shite but you never know how half a dozen pints might change things.

LIVELINE

'So your Yorkshire terrier, Snowy, climbed aboard the Mullingar train to Dublin and hasn't been seen since. Go ahead caller.'

For years now, every weekday between 1.45 and 3.00pm, Joe Duffy and his Liveline Army have been listening to the nation's people as they tell their stories, give their opinions, air their grievances and tell his listeners that *'it is a disgrace Joe; I mean it's an absolute disgrace'*.

Sometimes it goes horribly wrong and the economy of the country almost collapses after Mary rings in to say she has emptied her savings account because she no longer trusts the banks and Joe responds by saying *'I'm not surprised Mary, go on'*, sending 30,000 pensioners down to Main Street to do the same. And sometimes he allows some old fella to say something so utterly controversial (generally involving babies, communion, confessional boxes or Roy Keane) that the nation's telephone network melts. However despite the occasional faux pas, Liveline is often the only place that Jim and Joan Public can ring and get some support when all else fails.

Like what they said in the A-Team, *'if you have a problem ... if no one else can help ... and if you can find them ... maybe you can ring ... Liveline.'*

⚡ The airline told you to stand when you arrived with your 97-year-old grandmother?! Call Joe.

⚡ Someone just robbed your car with all your tools in the back of it?! Call Joe.

⚡ You were told to feck off by the manager when you asked for low-fat milk?! Call Joe.

⚡ Snowy is on the train to Dublin?! Call Joe.

And lo and behold, 30 minutes later the airline will have rung in to say it was a misunderstanding and that they will fly the pair all-expenses-paid to Lourdes; Mark, a taxi driver from Drimnagh, will have spotted and be parked behind your stolen car in Rathgar with the Gardaí already on their way; the café manager will be on with a pair of tickets for the opera and one hell of an apology; and Snowy will have been found safe and well and will be in the process of boarding the 15.05 train back out of Connolly.

Remember, just call Joe.

RiVERDANCE

While quite technical, Irish step-dancing basically involves both man and woman keeping their hands down by their sides, stiffening their upper bodies and kicking out in front and behind them. While somewhat impressive, it makes the dancer utterly unapproachable to a member of the opposite sex and impossible to chat up without risking injury.

At best you could call it an artistic form of defence; at worse, a contraceptive.

THEN CAME RiVERDANCE.

It was only meant to be a Eurovision interval act to keep the audience occupied and the viewers at home switched on. Gerry Ryan, wearing a ferocious yellow jacket, and Cynthia Ní Mhurchú announced something about a uniquely Irish performance that made mothers leave the kettle boiling to see what would happen next.

As the nation wondered, a ghostly woman appeared and sang something haunting in Irish that sent hairs up on necks and the cat running for cover. Then came two Irish-American step-dancers, all liberated with their hair done up and clothes hanging off them. They represented the river and the earth and probably the pent-up sexual frustration of early '90s Ireland.

To the steadily increasing beat of a drum and a rock-rhythm section they started getting it on, step-dance style, rising the blood across the land. As the dance continued, the tempo quickened, the whole country remained glued to their TVs and then it happened. The whole stage was on fire with dancers and kicking legs – ten, then twenty, then maybe a hundred charging to the front, towards the cameras, the music pumping, the water woman and the earth man leading them in a frenzy of lust and desire and God knows what, and the crowd went bananas!

And across the country of Ireland, children were sent to bed, mother and fathers tore the clothes off each other, kettles continued to boil and nine months later a generation of Eurovision Riverdance babies came into the world.

Irish step-dancing would never be the same again.

THE LATE LATE SHOW

≷ 'To whom it may concern.' ≷
≷ 'Roll it there Roisín.' ≷
≷ 'And there's one for everyone in the audience.' ≷

Three phrases that can only mean one thing: Friday night television and 'The Late Late Show'.

'The Late Late Show' is an Irish institution so influential that for over 50 years it has kept large parts of the population out of the pub on a Friday!

While the programme may have lost some of its gravitas, for more than two generations the show was a colossus of Irish TV. In its heyday it could command viewing audiences of close to a million people and had guests that ranged from Mother Teresa to Oliver Reed and breaking bands from U2 to Boyzone (will we ever forget their dance?!)

What made 'The Late Late Show' great, however, was not its varied guests or its Toy Show but those rare but beautiful occasions when it raised ground-breaking issues that drove conservative Ireland bananas, particularly the Church. Condoms, transparent nighties and lesbian ex-nuns were among the issues that came up for discussion, leading to letters of complaint rolling in as societal change rolled out.

When people think of 'The Late Late Show', many still remember Gay Byrne, the pucker-faced part-time grouch who anchored it for over 35 years (a world record for a chat-show host). Gay, or Uncle Gaybo as he was known, was a true professional though at times could rub the viewer up the wrong way.

Part of this was that he was unafraid to challenge orthodoxy, making many a little jealous. Part of this was also the way he would dispense with spotty-faced teenagers who pretended to be their Dads as their sisters ran down the fields in search of them. Uncle Gaybo had a no-nonsense approach to phone quizzes and unless he spoke to the name on the back of the postcard, you could forget it. He didn't hang around either and by the time Dad came in from pulling calves, Gaybo would have moved onto some family in Foxrock, telling them they were now going to Florida as the Fogartys from Fermoy were left to bemoan the fact that they would have to spend another summer break in Tramore.

Of course we still miss him now he's gone.

LOCK-iNS

It's well past three, the lights are low and voices hush as ears strain to hear if it is a knock on the door or just the wind. Shoulders tense, eyes scatter and pints settle. It can only be a lock-in.

Every so often if you are in the right place at the right time, the bar will shut, the doors will close and you and your friends will still be inside. Like a long delayed encore the barmen will re-appear, take to the high stools and only revisit to top up the drinks.

Maybe it's the after-hours taste of the stout that does it or the greater colour to the conversation, but time speeds up and before you know it, it's already dawn, one of your friends is asleep in the corner and you know you won't be making it to mass.

IRiSH FATHERS

THiNGS IRiSH FATHERS SAY TO THEiR SONS:

— *'If I have to come up to you!'*

— *'We're cutting turf this weekend.'*

— *'What you mean you've got something else planned?! Well un-plan it Einstein 'cos we're all going.'*

— *'Over-paid primadonnas if you ask me'* (no one asked him).

— *'Don't speak to your* (input as necessary) *like that!'*

— *'You're not watching that feckin' eejit, are ya?'*

— *'I picked it up in Lidls.'*

— *'Tell your Mam I'll just finish this and I'll be in for tea.'*

— *'Ffffor feck's sake, what you mean you failed geography? What are they teaching ya up there at all?!'*

— *'She's a fine girdle'* (on meeting your new girlfriend).

— *'What you mean you broke up with her?!'*

— *'Well you're some bollocks/gobshite/genius!'* (all negative).

— *'Is that what you call work?!'*

— *'Fair play to ya'* (congratulating on any award from a university degree to an All-Star).

— *'Well it's about time'* (congratulating on engagements).

THiNGS IRiSH FATHERS SAY TO THEiR DAUGHTERS:

◆ *'Do you want me to check it for oil?'*

◆ *'Ask your mother.'*

◆ *'You're not going out in that, are ya?!'*

◆ *'Ask your mother.'*

◆ *'You're my ol' pet/little daisy/shegozzah.'*

◆ *'Ask your mother.'*

◆ *'Will you turn over there to the news?'*

◆ *'Ask your mother.'*

◆ *'If you ask me, he's not good enough for you'* (no one asked him).

◆ *'Ask your mother.'*

◆ *'You're pregnant?!'*

◆ *'Does your mother know?'*

'GOiNG OUT' AND 'GOiNG OUT-OUT'

To compare 'going out' and 'going out-out' is akin to comparing the New Testament with the Old, full-fat milk with skimmed, or Westlife with Brian McFadden solo. They are just two very different things entirely.

Of course any good parent will tell you this, hence their age-old question to their children: *'are you going out or are you going out-out?'*

'Going out' is like going to the shops, taking the dog for a walk or seeing if your mate Steve is around.

'Going out-out' is an entirely different thing altogether. It is an activity that for men begins with them showering, shaving and spraying on both deodorant and anti-perspirant. For women, it is a process that starts with leg-shaving and finishes with fake tan, lasting anywhere between 45 minutes and two days.

After that both sexes are ready and can begin the main part of 'going out-out', which will commence 'in town' and will likely result in them losing their house key, ringing their ex at three in the morning, falling into the neighbours' hedgerow and looking forward to a world of pain the next morning.

That is why, if you respond by saying you are 'going out-out', parents sign off with a disclaimer that goes something in the way of *'well for heaven's sake look after your younger brother and remember, mass tomorrow is at 10'*.

While if you are just 'going out', they usually just ask you to pick up some milk on the way home.

SUNNY SPELLS AND SCATTERED SHOWERS

Sunny spells and scattered showers: sponsoring Irish weather since the Neolithics.

To an outsider, Ireland's nightly weather forecast might sound like a gambler betting both ways: *'it's either going to rain or be sunny tomorrow'*. However to an Irish person, hearing Gerry Fleming tell the viewers at home to expect *'sunny spells and scattered showers'* is like a warm duvet of stability in a weather world gone mad.

The comedian Bob Hope is meant to have once said that *'if you don't like the weather in Ireland, hang around 10 minutes'*. Sunny spells and scattered showers is that weather: the weather that sends you out to a football match with an umbrella and then brings you home with a tan and that waits for you to unpack the car boot for a picnic and then returns you that evening with the flu.

SUNDAY LUNCH

Roast meat, roast spuds, roast vegetables, roast stuffing, roast jugs of orange cordial, roast lots of stuff.

SUNDAY LUNCHES: A FAMILY TRADITION.

It doesn't matter if you haven't seen a potato all week between your pumpkin ravioli with sage butter on the Monday and quinoa with grilled zucchini and garbanzo beans on the Friday, nor whether you now live in Australia, Athlone or at college, when it comes to the weekend the traditional Sunday roast lunch still reigns supreme.

It's a time when you hold off talking about politics for one day and instead talk about who has died, got married or had kids since you were last home.

And if everyone behaves themselves then there may even be a bit of apple tart and raspberry ice-cream to finish.

HURLiNG

It is almost impossible to explain hurling. Encyclopaedias have spent years trying to draft an entry only to be left with something that sounds like one clan's violent act of retribution against another. I mean, 30 men, 30 sticks, a ball of leather, a hundred miles an hour, blood, sweat and tears?

So if you do want to describe hurling, you probably need to do so in a more circuitous way.

You need to explain that hurling is as much a language as it is a sport. We might all be able to pick up a few greetings in a foreign tongue, work hard be able to communicate, immerse ourselves to become fluent but only by being born into a language do you have the ability to be a true master of the spoken word. So it is with hurling. Only when you grow up without really understanding that there is a difference between a limb and a stick of ash can you become a true king at it.

You need to compare a hurling match to a poem and explain that instead of words, the player use hurls and instead of such things as metaphors, similes and sibilance, they use shots, scores and passes to spin verses full and rhymes rich with imagery that make up the 70 minutes of a Championship game.

You need to see the hurling championships as a Pulitzer Prize-winning novel with characters that we know, love, hate and love again. With a setting that feels like we've already been here before and a plot so complex and utterly absorbing that on the one hand we don't want it to ever end but on the other we know that either us or them or all of us will never make it through the winter if it doesn't.

And you need to see an All-Ireland winning team as a Michelin-star meal whose ingredients were sourced many miles from its final serving, whose spices and sauces took the most intricate routines to prepare, and whose fusion of tastes only comes to its wonderful culmination just moments before it appears in front of the palate of its audience in the cauldron that is a Croke Park or a Semple Stadium.

And even then that probably doesn't do hurling justice.

DRYING THE DISHES

For years there were households in Ireland where children had to commit to at least one piece of weekly housework. It was their sacrifice to show their appreciation for the week's work that traditionally had been done by Irish mothers who would wash, cook, clean, vacuum, iron, sew, dust, douse, extinguish, suture, strap, bandage, sooth, discombobulate, etc. It was also done because they had no other choice.

Long before the advent of dishwashers this piece of housework was the Sunday lunch wash-up. While it was a task that no child enjoyed, there was one part of it that was particularly torturous and would lead to resentment that would endure for years. It was known as the 'drying the dishes'.

The 'drying the dishes' was the cotton-picking, chimney-sweeping, canary-down-a-coal-mine of the Irish family household wash-up. No one wanted to do it so it fell to the second-born.

Cruelly it would also remain with the second-born even when they had left for college and the third, fourth, fifth, sixth and even seventh child had arrived. It was their task and their task alone. Any ideas that maybe the others who had now turned thirteen might take a turn or, heaven forbid, we let them '*air-dry*' were quickly met by '*will you quit complaining, sure haven't I been doing the ironing, vacuuming, cooking, cleaning, etc. all week?*' And with that retort the second-born would fall silent, take up the already damp dishcloth and begin.

But he or she would never forget. Years later when the first-born got the farm, took over as TD or began running the family shop, it remained the 'drying the dishes' that the second-born still resented the most.

THE RTÉ

Admittedly it is not the BBC. And yes it may, at times, have been prepared to spend more money on Pat Kenny's hair than on its London studio and steadfastly refused to produce a decent Irish comedy. But at least it is ours.

There were the highs: Mícheál Ó Muircheartaigh; the Angelus; Myles Dungan's Monday night Serie A football from a Portakabin; 'Nationwide'; 'Love/Hate', and Anne Doyle. There were the lows: Charlie Bird in a hotel room somewhere in Kuwait; most of its daytime chat shows; 'Leave it to Mrs O'Brien'; and 'Kenny Live'. And then there were those that lay somewhere in between – I mean, 'The Lyrics Board' anyone?!

Going live on radio in 1926 and on television in 1961, RTÉ (Raidió Teilifís Éireann) is one of the world's oldest public broadcasters and for many a long winter provided the main source of entertainment for the Irish public, particularly those who lived in what was then termed as 'two-channel land'.

NOT BEING ABLE TO TAKE A COMPLIMENT

Ireland's modesty knows no bounds. So much so that we are pathologically unable to accept compliments. This can be observed in the range of set responses we give to any words of praise, admiration or accolade.

FOR EXAMPLE:

Compliment: '*I love your top*'.
Response: '*What?! This old yolk?! I have it years.*' (She bought it yesterday.)

Compliment: '*Nice car.*'
Response: '*It's a hoor on the petrol.*' (It's the most economical car in its class.)

Compliment: '*What did you do with your hair? It looks great.*'
Response: '*Sure I only washed it!*' (The highlights cost more than a hundred euro.)

Compliment: *'Nice dress!'*
Response: *'Penney's, €5!'* (Marks and Spencer, €80.)

Compliment: *'Your son was awful nice helping me with all my groceries.'*
Response: *'Don't let him fool you.'* (He's the best son in the world and better than your lazy shite.)

Compliment: *'That was a great result for your daughter.'*
Response: *'I wish she was as good at cleaning her room.'* (Yes, she is wonderful.)

Compliment: *'I love your house.'*
Response: *'It's a mess, I haven't cleaned it in days!'* (I cleaned it for four hours before you came.)

Compliment: *'Thanks for the tea and the carrot cake infused with ginger and vanilla.'*
Response: *'It's nothing fancy – had I known you were coming over.'* (I knew you were coming.)

Compliment: *'This food is great.'*
Response: *'Really? I just threw it all in a pot.'* (My grandmother's recipe. The artichokes cost more than your coat.)

CHIPPER CHIPS

THERE ARE FRIES, THERE ARE CHIPS ...
AND THEN THERE ARE CHIPPER CHIPS.

When it comes to eating potatoes chopped roughly and cooked in oil, chipper chips have few equals, whether that be in taste or calorie content.

Legend has it that chipper chips only arrived in Ireland through a quirk in fate when Italian immigrant Giuseppe Cervi stepped off an American-bound boat in Cork. By the time he realised he had gotten off a stop and an ocean early, the boat had left and he was stuck behind in Ireland.

Legend tells that it was frying fish and chestnuts that he tried first, and this only turned to chips when he dropped a potato into the mix and the locals loved it. While Ireland isn't alone in its love of chipper chips, what I believe sets ours apart is that quick burst of Saxa table salt you always get along with the all-important washing-up-liquid bottle of vinegar, used to drown said chipper chips.

GUiNNESS

Guinness is one of the most renowned cultural icons of Ireland and the country's fourth most popular drink after water, milk and tae. To better understand this seminal drink a semi-fictitious timeline should help.

1759: Struck by the fact that the Irish people are not drinking enough, Arthur Guinness signs a 900,000-year lease at the St James Gate Brewery for a penny a year. He develops a porter and an ale. Local brewers reckon it is too expensive, too consistent and will never catch on.

1779: There are feck all local brewers left and Guinness now dominates the market.

1800: People drink Guinness, sales soar. Someone decides it is a good idea to export abroad.

1850: The toucan is invented.

1886: First US President drinks a pint of Guinness. From then on in, drinking a pint of Guinness becomes an election necessity to shore up the Irish-American vote.

1910: Guinness' attempt to make it onto the food pyramid narrowly fails, as carbohydrates vote against them.

1926: Medical breakthrough as it is discovered Guinness is actually good for you and doctors start to prescribe to patients. It is particularly good for those who are suffering from anaemia and are not getting enough iron. Shares in spinach plummet.

1944: Brief religious controversy takes place when a bishop suggests using Guinness as a substitute for unleavened bread during communion as war rationing continues. Voted down at Congress.

1962: Wide celebrations take place as Ireland and Nigeria celebrate a hundred years of close cultural bonds by opening a Guinness Brewery in Lagos. By the end of the 1970s, Nigeria will for a spell house the world's largest Guinness brewery and by the end of the millennium be the only place outside Dundalk where people can still be observed drinking Guinness' Harp Larger.

1977: Two barmen escape jail after pleading guilty to pouring Guinness at an angle of 48 degrees instead of 45 degrees, and for taking 155 seconds instead of the mandatory 119.5 seconds. In giving a suspended sentence the judge remarked that it was an honest mistake before adding '*good things come to those who wait*'.

2003: 4th International Panel of Climate Change Scientists rows back on earlier suggestion that Guinness drinkers are a significant factor in the release of greenhouse gases and global warming, second only to dairy cows.

2009: Archaeological digs reveal Arthur Guinness also had a role in getting rid of the snakes from Ireland. As a result he joins St Patrick in getting his own national day.

2013: Guinness's phenomenal marketing campaign scores another success when it becomes the first official drinks sponsor of a temperance movement.

TODAY: At exactly 17.59 someone sits down at a bar with a one-eyed collie-cross, the *Irish Times* and the smell of a ham and cheese toastie. He sits looking at the a pint of plain slowly settling in front of him, allowing the stress of the day roll off his shoulders, something that is completed with the placement of the cool dark pint of Guinness stout in front of him. The one-eyed collie-cross, probably called Lass, lies contently at his feet as the evening sun shines in.

MR FREEZE

When it comes to 'impossible to open without cutting your tongue, chipping your teeth or spilling some down your shirt' things, few items can compare to the Mr Freeze ice-pop, coloured flavoured frozen ice laminated in the same plastic packaging that butchers use for sealing rashers.

There were three ways to consume a Mr Freeze:

1. The first was by simply pushing up and eating the flavoured frozen ice inch after inch.

2. The second was by crushing the ice to help melt it. This then allowed you to drink its now cool contents. Allowing it to melt before opening it, however, exponentially increased the odds of half it ending on your t-shirt.

3. The last was to suck it straight, drawing out its sweet coloured contents to leave behind ice that then meets the same fate as the plastic packaging: the bin. Those who took this approach would years later go on to buy SUVs and lobby for the re-introduction of styrofoam burger packaging.

BED & BREAKFASTS

Bed & Breakfasts, or B&Bs, are the home from homes of Irish tourism. Slightly yet unexplainably more expensive than your average hotel room, they are places you go when you want to go on holiday but still want to feel like you are living at home.

There are several key characteristics that make up a proper B&B:

> They are run by women who remind you of every Irish mother.

> You will be asked within ten minutes of arrival, *'so you'll have a fry in the morning?'*

> You will have a great view from your bedroom window over the Irish countryside that you know would look spectacular if it stopped raining.

> The owners will commiserate with you that the weather has turned poor but *'had you been here last weekend'*.

- There will be at least seven photographs of their children, six photographs of their children's children and one of themselves when they first got married.

- You would not have recognised them from their wedding photograph.

- You will be expected to engage in at least two conversations about how their eldest is doing in Australia and how their daughter is just down the road but who calls up with the grandkids.

- They will have a lovely dog outside who *'doesn't bite'*, irrespective of whether he bites or not.

- They will have to explain to you how the shower works.

- You will have to ask again.

- The woman will be faintly racist but in an entirely good-natured way.

- The man will rarely leave the kitchen.

- They will know a taxi driver if you need to get a lift back from town later.

- The taxi driver will be their neighbour.

- If you are a couple, you will be guaranteed a room beside, above or below the owners.

- There will always be a sheepish-looking young man down late for breakfast. (He'll be looking sheepish as he can't remember if he actually managed to find the bathroom last night or peed into a pot plant.)

- You will be asked *'so how'd you get on last night?'* when the tea is brought out, and the length of questioning will depend on how hungover you are.

- The glasses they use for orange juice will be baby-sized.

- They will not take credit card.

Finally while there are several key characteristics that make up a proper B&B, there is only one true litmus test between a decent B&B and a great one: whether they use real Kellogg's Cornflakes and Rice Krispies at breakfast or some value-brand imposter.

THE FULL IRISH

While there are unhealthier options you can eat for breakfast (pure lard or strychnine being just two), there are very few that taste as good as a full Irish breakfast. The full Irish generally must consist of the following:

- Two sausages
- Two rashers
- One black pudding
- One white pudding
- One fried egg
- One fried tomato (sliced in half)
- Toast
- Brown bread
- A.N. Other (depending on county)
- And, last but not least, one large steaming pot of tea (to be pronounced 'tae')

Athough it is called a breakfast, the full Irish is amongst a very select band of world foods that can be eaten at any time throughout the day (the other two obviously being cornflakes and pizza).

NEUTRALITY

While this concept might sound strange to anyone who has ever stood outside Supermacs at three o'clock in the morning, Ireland has had a long and proud history of neutrality.

Our decision to remain neutral, decided shortly after independence, was perhaps partly driven by the hangover caused by 800-odd years of colonisation and a bloody civil conflict and partly due to our terrible record when it came to war:

PLAYED: 30
WON: 0
LOST: 29
DREW: 1

This neutrality was almost immediately tested during World War II when Winston Churchill gave the Irish a huge amount of stick for what he considered our *frolic with the Germans*'. Such criticism would rightly increase afterwards when the Taoiseach of the time, Eamon de Valera, offered his sympathies to the German ambassador on the death of Hitler; I mean, how must that letter have begun?!

'Dear German Embassy,
It was with deepest sympathy that I have heard of the demise of your totalitarian, anti-Semitic, crazed, evil, homicidal, sociopathic, one-balled dictator. While I never knew Adolf personally, as a fellow dog lover ...'

I mean, really?! Of course while De Valera may have gone too far in presenting a façade of 100% neutrality, Ireland's neutrality in World War II was much like a vegetarian who eats fish.

If German pilots ended up landing on Irish soil, they remained here as 'guests of the nation'. However if any Allied troops came down, doors were left unlocked and they tiptoed across the border with the north to re-join the war effort.

Our biggest contribution to the Allied war effort was our continuing fascination with crap weather. With Europe's only land-based observation station where readings on the

Atlantic's weather systems could be professionally taken, Ireland continued to feed its weather reports over to London. When we say Ireland though, it is perhaps as accurate to say Ted Sweeney, who on 3 June 1944 sent a weather warning that there was a *'Force 6 wind and a rapidly falling barometer'*. In Irish speak, it was *'going to turn nasty, boy'*.

He would be asked later to repeat this several times and as a result General Eisenhower put back the D-Day landings a day so the worst of the weather could pass and the Allies could successfully land at Normandy. The rest, as they say, is history.

BEGRUDGERY

Ireland has a superb system developed to help assist people overcome success, wealth, fame or fortune by reminding them that before they did well, they were just like us. It is a system that helps everyone keep one foot on the ground, two if possible, and that supports celebrities, heroes and champions in remembering their roots and not getting too far ahead of themselves, all the while helping the rest of us feel better for not succeeding. It is system that we call 'begrudgery'.

There are effectively five categories of begrudgery, which can be used for both men and women:

1. THE 'AND LOOK WHERE THAT GOT HiM' TYPE OF BEGRUDGERY:

This form is most often employed for those people who have completed an outstanding feat of bravery, like climbing up a tree to rescue a kitten, running into a burning building to save a child or taking a bullet for the President. The 'and look where that got him' refers to the fact that the hero no longer has a right index finger due to the little moggy, is permanently bald as a result of the blaze or is in fact dead.

2. THE 'I HOPE HE BREAKS HIS LEG' TYPE OF BEGRUDGERY:

This type of begrudgery is used for those people who were never particularly liked in the first place but who have now come into some unexpected good fortune, such as winning the Lotto, taking home a car in a raffle or having a claim come through for their 'bad' back. It is also used for the smug-looking young git who has just won that TV talent show but clearly has no manners. Due to the aforementioned young git's age, '*I hope he breaks his leg*' is employed instead of something stronger such as '*I hope he comes down with Ebola*'.

3. THE 'BUT SURE DIDN'T HIS WIFE LEAVE HIM' BEGRUDGERY:

This form comes into usage for people who have worked terribly hard, thus resulting in well-earned success, such as opening up a new business, receiving an entrepreneurial award or getting elected to public office. It generally signifies that the person saying '*but sure didn't his wife leave him*' could have achieved just the same amount success but they choose not to risk their marriage, irrespective of the fact that they may not even be married in the first place.

4. THE 'SURE HE'S PROBABLY ON DRUGS' BEGRUDGERY:

This variety tends to be strictly limited to someone who has triumphed in the sporting arena. It is employed irrespective of the fact that the winner may have been infuriatingly close to a medal for the last half a dozen years. Once they finally get gold, the fact that they are Irish, that they are from just down the road, that you beat them once in an U-10 football Feis Cup final and that it's not you who is now standing up on the Olympic podium is sure-fire evidence that *'sure he's probably on drugs'*.

5. THE 'SURE HE'S ONLY A BOLLIX' BEGRUDGERY:

This final form of begrudgery is strictly limited to people who have done well and who are 100% genuine, lovely, nice human beings. It is because these people are of such great character and spirit, have absolutely no blot on their soul and are the closest thing on earth we have to living angels that the only form of begrudgery that is relevant is the one that has absolutely no relevance, hence *'sure he's only a bollix'*. Individuals like Gandhi, Martin Luther King and Daniel O'Donnell spring to mind for this form of begrudgery. (Of course because the former two gave up their lives for their beliefs, they now of course fall into *'and look where that got him'* category.)

'AN BHFUiL CEAD AGAM DUL GO DTÍ AN LEiTHREAS?'

For years, the only Irish many children came out of school knowing was the expression, *'an bhfuil cead agam dul go dtí on leithreas?'* (Can I go to the toilet?)

While its usage varied from place to place – *'an bhfuil cead agam dul amach?'* (Can I go outside?) for those rural places were the toilet was behind a bush outside; *'más é do thoil é'* (please) for politer middle-class neighbourhoods – it was a phrase we all knew. And to this day, it is not only used in classrooms but also by footballers miming the national anthem, Irish backpackers trying to impress new foreign friends and what the average Irish adult considers sufficient knowledge to warrant ticking the 'Reasonably Fluent at Irish' box on the Census form.

CHEESE

Unbeknownst to a large swathe of the Irish public, during the late '80s and early '90s a bitter turf war was taking place in the lunchboxes of school-children across the country. While today we might bask in an array of wonderful cheeses from Abbey Smoked Brie to Knockatee Gouda as a benefit of our mild wet climate, back then it was a straight shoot-out between EasiSingles and cheddar for what lay between our sandwiches.

EasiSingles were exactly that: easy and single. With the time ticking down to the school bus, your Mam could slip the single out of its protective coat and onto the sandwich in seconds and have you on your way. In the other corner was cheddar, which needed a bit of time or you'd end up with chunks so thick they looked like book-ends between your sandwich, often preventing you from properly closing your lunch-box lid.

The divide between EasiSingles and cheddar tested many a friendship. However by the mid-1990s questions started to arise: while they may have been orange, were EasiSingles actually cheese? It was a controversy EasiSingles would never recover from and it marked the beginning of the end for the Singles.

THE IRISH PASSPORT

There is something deeply comforting about an Irish passport the closer you get to some alien immigration outpost.

Maybe it comes from the language the passport uses. While Britain and '*Her Britannic Majesty's Secretary of State Requests and requires in the Name of Her Majesty*' that all their citizens are allowed through and the US wants this to happen '*without delay*', the Irish passport just seems to give the sense of '*whenever you get the chance would you mind letting them in*'.

Whatever the reason, it is with confidence that we watch as the wary immigration officer first views you with suspicion as you hand over your document, and then with slight confusion as he tries to work out which county you belong to with a harp symbol out front and a big 'Éire' printed above. One of two things will happen. Either the immigration officer will remember a time he too was drunk and beam back at you '*you Irish, you're all alcoholics*' (India–Pakistan border 2002) before motioning you through or he will show your passport to his colleague who will confirm that yes, Ireland is indeed a real country before waving you onwards.

THE LEAVING CERT

Traditionally starting the first Wednesday of June, aka the hottest day of the year, the Leaving Certificate is the great leveller of Irish teenagers. It doesn't matter where your accent is from, what deodorant you use or if your mother still cuts your hair: if you score 600 points there's hardly a course in the state that won't accept you. Of course if you perform poorly, then you might want to think about keeping that school uniform for one more year.

At no other time of the year will there be as many prayers said by parents, candles lit by grandparents and promises to name their first-born Seamus, Sylvia or W.B. if their selected poet comes up.

Students who spent the spring updating their social status and deselecting Spurs players from their fantasy football teams congregate around exam centres (the locker room and the gym), crack jokes, look brave but deep down are scared shitless they'll be confronted by plate tectonics, the second inter-party coalition or the *Modh* feckin' *Coinníollach*!

It can be an awful time in a teenager's life that can linger for years later with instances known of 30-year-olds, who never had the faintest idea what X or Y were, found tossing and turning in bed before screaming out *'léigh anois go cúramach ar do scrúdpháipéar na treoracha agus na ceisteanna!'*

But for those of us who did make it, and who promptly forgot what a quadratic equation was and no longer cared if it was *'le'*, *'la'* or *'l'*, it is a bond that still ties us and that we remember every warm early June day.

BARMEN

Of course when we refer to barmen, we are not referring to those eejits who, after getting a solitary order of a Smithwicks and bottle of Coke, stare off into the middle distance so afraid are they that they'll make eye-contact with another customer and have to remember two orders at once.

No, when we refer to barmen, we refer to those men and women ...

... who don't charge you for water and a dash of MiWadi.

... who ask you how your day is going, at exactly the right time and not a moment sooner.

... who can lip-read your aura from 400 yards and know you don't want ice with your Paddy.

... who give you a nod when you arrive and a nod when you go.

... who have an umbilical relationship with their fellow barmen where they can start a pint pour and head down to change the kegs safe in the knowledge that their compadre has their back.

... who buy you a drink once a year and every so often reward you with a lock-in.

... who call you a taxi or drive you home because it's not like you to get 'that bad'.

... who don't hit on you every time you're having relationship trouble but instead tell you an obscenely hilarious joke they heard off an old man with dog half an hour ago.

... who turn up the TV for the analysis, turn it down for announcements and give it to you because yours is on the blink and sure they have to get a new one anyhow!

... who will make your sore throat and cold fingers a hot whiskey or port, even if it is annoying.

... who don't seem to see you during a Christmas crowd but, when you turn back around to the bar, have arrived down with your order and exact change because that what the job is.

... who can hold three pints and a packet of King crisps in one hand, take your money in another and pass you a glass of ice with a third.

... who are genuinely nice people who happen to sell alcohol.

STRAWBERRIES BY THE ROADSIDE

You are travelling at 100 km/h and then something flashes past you like a rumour. You won't be quite sure what it was but all of a sudden you begin to feel peckish.

Then, as an answer to a question you didn't know you had, you see it – a second sign: '*Irish Strawberries, New Potatoes*'. At this stage a maelstrom of feelings will hit you with the root wonder remaining the same: should you stop? The last sign makes up your mind: '*Wexford, 2 for €5, Queens, 200 metres*'.

In a trail of dust, chippings and gravel you decelerate in beside a movable trailer where a college student is reading a get-rich-quick book to the sound of passing traffic. You end up buying two punnets of strawberries, a bag of Queens and some gooseberries, even though you have no idea in what manner they should be consumed. Roll on the summer.

CHEERiNG ON OUR ENEMY'S ENEMY

Nothing says '*I'm Irish*' more that cheering on our enemy's enemy. Of course nowadays England are as much our enemy as Magneto or Ming the Merciless is. I mean, 800 years of colonisation and a famine aside, we support all their soccer teams, we watch all their programmes and listen to all their music. And if we met at a bar in a far-flung corner of the globe you can be sure we'd have a bloody good night out.

That said.

There is something innate that clicks in whenever England put on that white shirt, start singing 'God Save the Queen' and get ready for kick off that means you just can't help but cheer on their opponents, especially if that sport involves penalties.

LOOKERS ON

One quaint aspect of Irish life is that television interviews with people of note often take place in very public arenas, thus allowing anyone and his dog to pop up in the background. This is what you call a 'looker on'.

Lookers on can be roughly divided into nine different categories:

1. THE WAVERS: These individuals usually look square into the camera with an open type of grin and wave slowly, in the same way a collie dog might wave into outer space unsure if anyone is actually out there and will see them.

2. THE ON-THE-PHONERS: These are an evolved version of the wavers. Unwilling to take the chance that no one will see them, they ring up someone they know is doing nothing better than sitting at home in front of the television. They can be spotted in the background on the phone before turning to the camera and waving, certain their mate Dave is now watching. Confirmation of this comes in how they wave even stronger when Dave shouts back at them, '*Jaysus, I can see you, you're there behind them, on the TV!*'

3. THE ACTUALLY-INTERESTED-ERS: These individuals, usually over the age of 60 and possible unaware of the filming device, are genuinely interested in what the interviewer has to say and can be spotted craning an ear in the direction of the talker. If the interview goes on for more than five minutes, they will be visibly disappointed if they interviewer does not ask them a question.

4. THE KID WITH A HURL: While these characters will usually appear in the background of an interview taking place after a hurling match, they can turn up in any form of interview, from election count centres to multi-car collisions.

5. THE GUY WITH A KID ON HIS SHOULDERS: By having a child on their shoulders these lookers on are allowed to wrestle their way closer to camera, irrespective of the fact that they might not even know the kid on their shoulders.

6. THE STICK-YOUR-FINGER-UPPERS: These individuals, also known for defacing cubicle walls, will suddenly be overcome with an urge to stick their fingers up at the camera. They can also double up as an 'on-the-phoner', and in this case should be forgiven because while it might look like they are telling the whole viewing public to feck off, they are in fact just telling their mate Dave on the other end of the line.

7. THE WAIT-UNTIL-IT'S-OVER-ERS: These figures, usually under the age of twenty, lurk in the background waiting until the interview is over before letting out a huge roar that often begins with '*C'MON!*' before disappearing into noise.

8. THE NERVOUS LOOKERS ON: This group, representing the vast proportion of the population, will wander in and out of shot. Lacking the full confidence to stay the full interview, they would much rather be on someone's shoulders but, considering they are now in their thirties, realise this would just look weird.

9. THE GENUINELY-HAVEN'T-A-FECKIN'-CLUE-WHAT'S-GOING-ON-ERS: These individuals saw a crowd and have managed to wander right into shot. They are oblivious to everything and even after, when their school/college/work-mates tell them they saw them on the TV last night, will genuinely not know what they are talking about.

THE DEATH NOTICES

When people in Ireland argue about the print media era being over, what they sometimes fail to take into account are the death notices.

There is still a generation of Irish people who wake up every morning and buy the paper for the sole purpose of pouring over the death notices. Once they see they are not in it, they move on to see if anyone they know is. While websites such as the aptly named rip.ie and hourly local radio updates might help with the cross-referencing, there is nothing quite like the death notices and the dearly beloveds to help fill one's social calendar with reposals, removals and funerals. Once that is done, they are free to begin their daily chores.

THE IRISH SUMMER

While it might be a little harsh to say that Irish summers are usually as long as a mayfly's retirement, there is always genuine amazement when you meet someone overseas who tells you they were in Ireland last summer and the weather was wonderful! The reason for this as we all know is that in general Irish summers do not last long, are not very warm and are not even guaranteed.

That said, when they do arrive there is no greater place. Lawns get mowed on the hour, barbecue sets sell out, ice-cream sales go through the roof, shirts come off, spirits soar, skin burns and radio presenters promise that today is the day it's going to break 30°C!

Of course there will always be some who will start complaining after three days that it is '*fierce hot*', after five days that it is '*too hot*' and after a week to remind us of '*the farmers, sure their cattle are dying of thirst!*'. For the rest of us, if the summer spell lasts for more than a week it makes our year and if, heaven forbid, it stays for the fortnight then people will talk about it for a generation after, '*I mean, boy, the summer of '95, that was a scorcher!*'

THE DEN

Ireland usually lags behind the popular culture curve so it's nice to see when we do finally catch up that we take that little step further. And so it was with the arrival of Ireland's first real afternoon children's TV show, 'The Den'. Sure we had Bosco before it but 'The Den', or 'Dempsey's Den' as it was known in its original incarnation, really did bring Irish children's television programmes into the 20th century.

Presented first by Ian Dempsey and then Ray D'Arcy, the programme introduced a host of non-human human-like characters that included aliens Zig and Zag, Dustin the Turkey (saved from a Christmas dinner) and Podge, a psychopathic boy-like puppet to Irish television. The show, whose heyday lasted for well over a decade, pushed the boundaries of what was acceptable on children's television and the nation's children loved it. Perhaps the most famous example of this came when Zig and Zag implied that the then President of Ireland, Mary Robinson, had smelly feet. She happened to be in the studio with them at the time.

HB ICE-POPS

Long before over-priced Häagen-Dazs appeared in freezers, Ireland had a long and cherished history of ice-pops stemming from Hazelbrook Farm, or HB, ice-pops. We also had Dale Farm but they weren't as popular, due to the long unfounded association with Glasgow Rangers Football Club. HB had several well-known and beloved products:

❧ THE SUPER SPLIT ❧

The custard cream of the ice-pop world. A basic orange-flavoured ice over ice-cream, the Super Split's only fault was that the exposed ice-cream at the base of the ice-pop would always begin to melt before you were through with the half-inch of solid orange ice up top.

❧ THE CHOC ICE ❧

This was the working-man's Magnum before we even knew what Magnums were. With an ice-cream core faintly covered by chocolate, this was also an adult's ice-pop as they took the moral high ground by refusing to allow their tongues to become covered with colour.

✧ THE FAT FROG ✧

The Choc Ice's mortal enemy, the Fat Frog was everything the Choc Ice wasn't. It was green ice, scoffed at the idea of containing ice-cream and left your tongue utterly phosphorescent. Kids loved it.

✧ TANGLE TWISTER ✧

This was a Quaker-led peace-building ice-cream exercise that sought to bring unity between Choc-Icers and Fat-Froggers. It had ice-cream, it had green ice, it had red something. It didn't work.

✧ CALIPSO ✧

This ice-pop usually signified that you were a family who could afford to have a holiday overseas and/or owned a second car. (Its actual name was Calippo but only people who owned a second car knew this.)

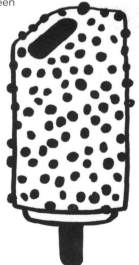

✧ BRUNCH ✧

Ireland's first gay-friendly ice-pop, a game-changer.

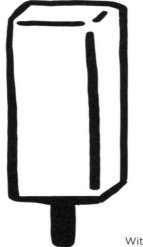

✂ GOLLY BAR ✂

A block of vanilla ice-cream whose only saving grace was that its wrapper was punctured by its stick, meaning it was almost impossible to unwrap. This allowed it to be withdrawn from the shelves before the Irish public realised what a ridiculously inappropriate name it had.

✂ LOOP THE LOOP ✂

With lime water ice, lemon sorbet and a chocolate topping, this was a favourite amongst free-thinkers, radicals, reggae fans and second-born members of the family.

✂ FREAKY FOOT ✂

This was the New Labour of ice-pops. It was basically a rebranded Raspberry Ripple in the shape of a foot with a chocolate-covered big toe. It fooled nobody.

✂ SPARKLER ✂

Pure orange ice-pop that was bought just before pay-days.

❧ CORNETTO ❧

Bought on pay-days or for special occasions such as engagements and funerals. If you saw a child on their own eating one of these in 1980s Ireland, there was a high likelihood that it was stolen.

❧ WIBBLY WOBBLY WONDER ❧

Pink strawberry- and yellow banana-flavoured ice-cream, with an upper half of frozen yellow lemon jelly coated in chocolate, the Wibbly Wobbly Wonder was one of the nation's favourites but was inexplicably taken off the shelves in 2000. Some people say it was because of the Y2K Millennium bug, others say because of the number of law-suits stemming from the jelly falling off the stick while still others say it was a prerequisite for us to join the EU single monetary policy. Whatever the reason, for years after many people still woke up on a sunny summer's day hoping to find Bobby Ewing from Dallas in their shower with a Wibbly Wobbly Wonder and realise it was all a dream. Unfortunately for them, it wasn't.

SPICE BURGERS

URBAN MYTHS ABOUT SPICE BURGERS:

- Someone in Longford discovered the recipe to spice burgers but Big Oil had them killed.

- There is a spice burger factory in Area 51.

- If you eat a spice burger standing up, you can't get pregnant.

- If you rub a spice burger on a scar, it will fix it.

- The Third Secret of Fatima was about spice burgers.

- A spice burger is the only man-made food that you can see from space.

- A spice burger shot JFK.

- Spice burgers are not on the food pyramid.

- You can kill a spice burger with a silver bullet.

- Spice burgers do not taste nice after three pints of anything.

- Irish people know the origin of spice burgers.

BRINGING HOME THE TURF

Every summer in many a household up and down the country a similar scene plays out:

7.45am: Mother shouts up the stairs to Son #1 that *'if you're not up and ready in the next five minutes you may forget about that holiday with your friends'*. She then turns to Son #2 and tells him to change out of those runners. *'It's not mass you're going to!'*

7.55am: Mother finishes smearing sun cream factor 50 on all involved, the car is boarded and the family head off to the bog.

7.58am: Son #1 realises that he has forgotten to bring the football to which Dad replies, *'you won't have time to play football'*. Meanwhile, Son #2 questions the whereabouts of his sister only to be told to *'never mind where your sister is'*.

9.00am: Arrive down the country at the bog and begin saving* the turf.

*Saving: the process whereby the damp side of turf is turned over and exposed to the wind and sun to help dry it. Level of back-breakingness: 8.5/10.

11.30am: Tea, sandwiches, stretch.

12.00pm: Mother re-applies sun cream factor 50, turning everyone's faces dirty brown with the light film of bog dirt that has previously built up. Everyone returns to work and begins the process of footing* the turf.

*Footing: the process whereby the reasonably dry turf is stacked in small towers to further help with the drying. Level of back-breakingness: 7/10.

2.30pm: Tea, sandwiches, stretch.

3.00pm: Mother re-applies sun cream factor 50, by now smearing a thick coat of black dust around everyone's entire faces. Everyone returns to work and begins the process of stacking* the turf.

*Stacking: the process whereby the dry turf is stacked into the waiting trailer or boot of the car so that every square inch is used. Level of back-breakingness: 6/10.

5.30pm: Depart bog and beg parents to '*stop in a shop*' on the way home.

6.30pm: Arrive home. Sons told that they '*may forget football training for this evening*' so they can help their Dad unload the turf. Level of back-breakingness: 8/10.

8.30pm: Job done, dinner on the table, sister on wash-up duty.

10.30pm: Sons fall asleep with exhaustion watching sports highlights. Have a ginormous sleep.

Repeat two weeks later and two weeks after that to the end of the season.

SHARING THE DEATHS

In Ireland social tradition dictates that it is the duty of the oldest member of a family to find out who's dead in the community and share this news onwards. This sharing generally follows a very strict ritual, more so when the person being told is a relative halfway across the world.

To begin with, the news must be shared as early in the conversation as possible, preferably following some positive news from the person who doesn't know, such as a graduation, a birth or a lottery win.

The conversation goes as follows:

Dad: *'Hello, Mary?'*
Mary: *'Hi Da, how are you?'*

Dad: *'Fine. How's Australia? What's the weather like?'*

Mary: *'Sunny, Da – it's Australia, it's always sunny. Da, I've got some news – me and Greg got engaged.'*

Dad: *'That's great, love. I'll tell your Ma. Pet, do you remember Páidí beag?'*

Mary: *'No, Da.'*

Dad: *'He was in your school, year below you. Lives up the road past the Kellys.'*

Mary: *'No, Da.'*

Dad: *'He used to play for the Junior B hurling team, along with your brother. He got sent off for biting that corner-back last two years ago in the final. Works as a carpenter in Dublin. Used to get the same bus as you in the morning.'*

Mary: *'No, Da.'*

Dad: *'He used to do the collection at mass. You'd see him bringing Ol' Mrs Duignan's shopping home every Friday.'*

Mary: *'Oh, hold on. Yeh, Páidí. Now I remember. Why?'*

Dad: *'Dead! Stone dead so he is! Tragic. They found him yesterday. He was crushed by a rabid cow. Awful like. Your Ma and I are going to removal this evening so we are.'*

Mary: *'Oh.'*

Dad: *'Alright love, well done on the engagement, I'll tell your Ma. Love you.'*

Mary: *'Thanks Da.'*

AER LiNGUS

Sure, they sometimes strike. And sure, it's all now online, impersonal and easier to find Bill Murray's cell number than their own. And sure, you might not get any change from a twenty if you buy a tea, a sandwich and packet of crisps. And sure, it is nearly all a private company anyway. And sure ... And sure ...

... BUT ...

... there is one thing about Aer Lingus that anyone who has ever gotten aboard one of their planes anywhere outside Ireland will tell you. When you sit down, buckle in and the cabin doors close, you know that you are on your way home to Ireland.

THE SNUG

Traditionally the snug was the part of the pub comfortably located towards the front, partitioned off from the rest of the bar. It was a place where women could come in to drink half-pints while avoiding the unwanted attention of the men-folk.

Thankfully that's now all changed as women can drink wherever the hell they want and anyone can sneak their way into what often is the cosiest part of the bar and a place where stories are spun, worries shared, hearts opened, old times recounted and a drink is only a knock on the sliding window away.

ROUNDERS

The most accurate way to describe the sport of rounders is that it is a more relaxed version of baseball with less stats and more craic. Other characteristics to this Irish sport that differentiate it from its American cousin include the following:

- Both boys and girls can play at the same time, something only one of my class-mates in primary school was mature enough to realise. (Unsurprisingly he would later become the first person I knew who dated girls.)

- Tennis balls work best and hurleys are used instead of baseball bats.

- If the person who is batting actually plays hurling, everyone fielding should move ten steps back.

- You throw the ball underarm so as to actually allow the person hit it, unless they are really, really crap. In this case, you may allow them to use a tennis racket.

- When you hit the ball, you must run while throwing the hurl wildly out behind you, narrowly missing the home catcher.

- Instead of throwing the ball at the base most likely to get a runner out, you are allowed panic and throw to home-base or at the person shouting loudest. No one will blame you.

- If the game involves players who are close to or over the age of thirty, someone will either 1) slip and muddy their new jeans, or 2) pull their calf muscle.

- The 'one-handed catch' is the crème de la crème of fielding as it gets the whole team out if executed correctly ...

- ... but it should never be tried when you only have one person left to get out.

- The winning team is the team that is in front when:

  - The barbecue is ready.
  - It begins to lash rain.
  - Someone pulls their calf muscle.

MÍCHEÁL Ó MUIRCHEARTAIGH

When it comes to sports commentary there are few who could compete with the great Mícheál Ó Muircheartaigh. Whereas some commentators sound like a GPS machine on steroids, Ó Muircheartaigh painted a picture so vividly that radio listeners at home would feel that at times they too were running alongside the players.

Ó Muircheartaigh seemed to know every GAA player personally and would often break into character background about a particular midfielder, telling us who their uncle played for, what their parents did, what the player liked to do in their spare time, and even what their parents liked to do in their spare time! As he would do all this, the ebbing and flowing intensity of his voice would dictate the player's position on the field and their threat to goal, meaning the audience at home were safe in the knowledge that they would not miss a thing.

What Ó Muircheartaigh, who retired in 2010 at the sprightly age of 79, was perhaps best loved for though was not these incidental details he'd colour his commentary with but for his other irreverent lines that are forever immortalised. Among our favourites are:

— *'Teddy looks at the ball, the ball looks at Teddy.'*

— *'Seán Óg Ó hAilpín, his father's from Fermanagh, his mother's from Fiji. Neither a hurling stronghold.'*

— *'Pat Fox has it on his hurl and is motoring well now, but here comes Joe Rabbitte hot on his tail ... I've seen it all now, a Rabbitte chasing a Fox around Croke Park!'*

— *'Anthony Lynch, the Cork corner-back, will be the last person to let you down – his people are undertakers.'*

— *'1–5 to 0–8 ... well, from Lapland to the Antarctic, that's level scores in any man's language.'*

— *'Teddy McCarthy to Mick McCarthy, no relation; Mick McCarthy back to Teddy McCarthy, still no relation.'*

— *'If the streaker doesn't mind, it will be going over his direction now.'*

— *'Colin Corkery on the 45 lets go with the right boot. It's over the bar. This man shouldn't be playing football. He's made an almost Lazarus-like recovery from a heart condition. Lazarus was a great man but he couldn't kick points like Colin Corkery.'*

— *'The stopwatch has stopped. It's up to God and the referee now. The referee is Pat Horan. God is God.'*

THE FRONT ROOM

'The Front Room' aka 'the Good Room' is the most sacred room in the Irish household. Characteristics of the front room include:

- No playing allowed.

- It is the only place in the house where crystal is visible.

- The only pictures allowed to hang are:
  - Wedding photos.
  - Graduation photos of older siblings and their children, leading younger siblings to believe that the only way they can be successful is if they move out.

- The parish priest has never visited any other room except this one.

- Your friends have visited every other room except this one.

- Its only other regular use is for welcoming relatives who are wealthier than you.

- It smells of books that you've never read and wild flowers.

- Shooting Granny is more forgivable than being caught in there with a football.

- The only occasion you will be allowed to sleep in the front room is if you are laid out in a coffin.

THE STRAY SOD

There are many folklore stories that describe strange goings-on in rural Ireland.

One of these stories is that of the 'stray sod'. This story involves a poor victim who is criss-crossing the myriad of hedge-rowed fields of Ireland stepping on what is called the 'stray sod'.

Once the stray sod is trodden upon, the poor soul would quickly find themselves lost, unable to find their way out of the field, wandering aimlessly sometimes for days until:

◆ They are found by a passer-by.

◆ They are able to draw attention to themselves through the use of a high-pitched scream, a gunshot or a smoke signal.

◆ They sober up.

'AH SURE'

'*Ah sure*': that wonderful multi-functional Irish phrase that tries to put a silver lining where little or none exists. Often heard in phrases such as:

'AH SURE ...

... *there's always next year.*'

... *you never liked him much anyway.* '

... *it will be better by the time you're married.* '

... *it can't rain forever.* '

... *at least it's not broken.* '

... *at least you don't use that one for writing.* '

... *you were never going to be a model/football player/ anyway.* '

... *it's only a suspended sentence, it's not like you can't visit America.* '

... *why would you want to visit America anyway?* '

... *worse things have happened at sea.* '

... *no one died.* '

... *only one person died.*'

SPREADING SLURRY

Few smells epitomise the Irish countryside more than the scent of spread slurry (cow's waste in layman's terms). You're driving along the Irish countryside with the windows down and the sun shining when a blast of slurry stench hits the car. As children in the back rush to blame each other, the driver is left to choose: should they roll the windows up in the vain hope of preventing further entry or just ride out the storm?

While slurry might mean that Irish 'Escape to the Country' television property programmes will never be complete without a wealthy retired city couple looking to relocate into nature wondering what the hell is that smell, slurry also indicates one thing: good weather fit for fertilising. And for that we can be grateful.

PENNEYS

THE EVOLUTION OF CLOTHES:

---- First came simple *homo sapiens* stripping bark off trees and wearing leaves.

---- Then there was the use of wool and the skin of dead animals.

---- Next arrived the domestic system where everything needed was made in the village.

---- After that came the Industrial Revolution.

---- And then finally there was Penneys.

Using the same factories as pretty much every other garment manufacturer but charging the customer less, Penneys has revolutionised the Irish clothing market making it now possible to comfortably outfit a family for €20 per person and still have money left for the bus fare home.

THE ANGELUS

BONG

For some, it is a reminder of the grip that Catholic Ireland once held on us; for others, it gives them a chance to catch the English six o'clock news headlines. For most however, the Angelus is simply a constant in Irish television in much the same way that the television is.

BONG

Every evening at six o'clock, the bells of St Mary's Pro-Cathedral ring out for a one-minute Angelus broadcast on the national channel, RTÉ 1.

BONG

With the exception of a minority who are looking for a quick hit as they continue to come down from early morning mass, the majority of the Angelus' 318,000 average daily audience is drawn from those who have tuned in for the Six One RTÉ News a minute early and are then caught help-lessly in an undertow of continuous bongs.

BONG

The Angelus has rarely changed since it hit the TV screens more than 60 years ago. Its biggest makeover came in 2009 when it went from a screenshot of a stained glass window or painting showing the Annunciation to video-grabs of multi-cultural Ireland with people who are either reflecting deeply on life or realising that they have forgotten to buy something from the local Centra but can't quite remember what it was.

BONG

This change was at the time so controversial it was thought to have caused a run on the banks, accelerated the recession and ousted the incumbent government.

BONG

While occasionally unpopular, cancellation of the Angelus has never been seriously considered and Ireland today is still closer to legalising crack cocaine than it is to getting rid of the Angelus.

BONG

IRISH WEDDINGS

TIPS FOR HAVING AN IRISH WEDDING:

♥ Expect the weather to be the absolute opposite of what you hoped for. (Best then to hope for torrential rain.)

♥ You need to have at least one 'drunk uncle' present. They will set the very bottom standard for what is appropriate and allow everyone else to work upwards.

♥ Beef or salmon?

♥ The married couple would be happier if you gave them herpes than another feckin' toaster.

♥ The priest is liable to do anything from going viral while singing to confusing the groom's name with your ex-boyfriend's. Whatever, it will be comedy gold.

♥ If in doubt, vol-au-vents.

♥ Wine for arriving guests as you are getting your photos taken – good. Whiskey for arriving guests as you are getting your photos taken – bad, very bad.

♥ Don't be afraid to be 'aunt-heavy' on your invite list. They will populate the dance-floor long before the younger ones have drunk enough to join them.

♥ 42 minutes and 17 seconds is always a safe bet for the speeches. If successful, buy a round and do not put the winnings in your pocket or no one will want to dance with you after.

♥ In 90% of cases, the band does not have to be very good. As long as they can go seamlessly from 'I'm Gonna Be (500 miles)' to '99 Red Balloons' and also play 'Sex on Fire' so the men can put their ties around the heads, link arms and dance, then you are sorted.

♥ If you get a photographer, expect to spend the equivalent of a small economy car on him.

♥ Best man speeches should not involve any of the following words: *'vomit'*, *'jail-time'*, *'never proven in court'*, *'sheep'*, *'substance abuse'* or *'Belgian roadside brothel'*.

♥ Expect at least one of your friends to dance entirely inappropriately with one of your aunts but don't worry as this will only come to light in the video afterwards.

♥ Finally there is no better way to end a wedding (for those not staying in the honeymoon suite) than to listen to someone usually from Munster singing a ballad about someone dying, emigrating or dying while they emigrate.

CEMETERY SUNDAYS

Every summer, on one specific Sunday, families across Ireland return to the graves of dead relatives and at first remember, then reminisce and then do what their now passed loved ones would really want them to be doing: catch up with their cousins, aunts and uncles who they haven't seen since the last wedding, funeral or Cemetery Sunday. If the weather is good, the rain holds off and the midges are not out in force, conversations on the latest engagement, graduation, birth or driving offence will be shared; the latest joke will be offered; and the county's chances in the Championship analysed.

In fact if it weren't for the first of ten Hail Marys in the first of three Blessed Rosaries, you could almost be having real fun. With the only craic for the next half hour coming from someone slipping of the edge of one grave stone and the priest throwing what seems like half glass of water over your older brother as he does the rounds, you must wait it out until the padre finally lets you go and the conversations either continue on in a nearby relation's house or in the pub, or both.

A SCHMOZZLE

A 'schmozzle' is somewhere on the spectrum between friendly thumps amongst friends and second degree assault.

It is generally only ever found in Gaelic games where 'fighting' does not take place. Instead, schmozzles occur. These events can arise for a number of reasons that range from being 3 goals and 12 points down with five minutes left on the clock to an opposing player enquiring into the marital status of your mother at the time of your birth.

To an outsider, it may appear that blood and bones are being spilt and split. However to anyone involved in Gaelic games, it is just a giant form of 'handbags' involving anywhere from three to 30 players. Finally it is important not to confuse a 'schmozzle' with an 'almighty schmozzle', which will also include the subs bench, managing staff, an *Maor Uisce*, several members of the crowd and, if it is a Junior B hurling match, a collie-cross barking.

POITÍN

Poitín: A traditionally illicit alcohol product produced in a small pot or still using potatoes, sugar beet, barley, treacle or whatever you're having yourself.

SOME FACTS ABOUT POITÍN:

- It seems to somehow always come into your family either from your uncle, from someone visiting from Clare or from your uncle visiting from Clare.

- Your parents never have poitín in the house, unless someone suffers a terrible shock when it will then magically appear. It has to be a *terrible* shock however. If it is merely a *bad* shock, then whiskey will suffice.

- While poitín was originally made to drink, there are several others uses for it including:
  - Back-ache
  - Ear-ache
  - Head-ache
  - Muscle-ache

- Heart-ache
- Ache
- Curing any ailment a calf may have, up to and sometimes including death
- Paint-stripping

🍶 While no one has ever met them, there is supposedly a whole sub-culture of bachelor farmers who have gone blind drinking it.

🍶 Poitín has recently been granted Geographical Indicative Status by the EU, meaning it must be produced in Ireland to be called poitín, in the same way Champagne, Parma ham and Parmesan cheese must all come from certain areas too. Not bad for something used to de-ice engines.

🍶 In the olden days, images of the Gardaí knocking over barrels of poitín into a mucky farmer's yard made for great news and were like the Irish version of 'Cops'.

🍶 Nowadays poitín can be bought in shops, something that would make blind farmers from Clare turn in their graves if they knew it was going on.

THE COMMUNITY GAMES

While it may never make the CV, qualifying for the Community Games finals in Mosney is many a young child's dream growing up and often one of their proudest moments.

The Community Games are quite simply the Olympic Games for Irish children, first organised in 1967 to give children something to do other than sniff glue and set fire to things. Proving immediately popular, the Games quickly grew from 5,000 participants in its inaugural year to the half a million who compete today, all in the hope that they might make it to Mosney, County Meath, and follow in the footsteps of such notables as Sonia O'Sullivan, Niall Quinn, Tommy Bowe and er ... Jedward.

While the final location may have changed from Mosney, the spirit and breath of the games has not. This is because the Community Games has always been more than a 100-metre sprint. With a spectrum of events that ranges from skittles to pitch 'n' putt, disco-dancing to throwball, hand-writing to something titled 'project', it continues to give crap kids the chance to have the same dreams as all the fit, fast and more skilful children.

That said, I never made it past the county art final when I discovered that tracing paper and a newspaper cut-out were not permissible in open competition, reducing my Mosney dreams to ashes.

STINGER BARS (AND THEIR FRIENDS)

While this book has resisted the urge to include 'bad teeth' as a reason to love Ireland, it cannot hide from one of the reasons for our occasional bad teeth: the sweet chew bars of the '80s and '90s that made it possible.

OUR TOP 9:

9 (& 8).

Dennis the Menace and Desperate Dan: Outwardly the more English option, they were able to navigate Irish sweet shops by flying under the comic book flag. Dennis the Menaces were black and red with little other information given, while the Desperate Dan was a ridiculous 'orange'-flavoured chew with black crystals, something I realised years later were meant to symbolise Dan's stubble.

7.

Drumsticks: A raspberry and milk-flavoured chew on the end of a stick. Would later become a bar and meet the same fate as the Refresher (see below).

6.

Woppa: A spearmint-flavoured bar whose taste could almost make you believe that it was a sweet way of washing your teeth. There was also a cola version that, while also costing 5p, you just knew was a poor man's Woppa.

5.

Roy of the Rovers: A luminous yellow bar whose colour alone should have had alarm bells ringing in parents' ears. Stuck to your teeth like a Melchester Rovers blanket defence, a reference you'd get if you read Roy of the Rovers.

4.

Tangy: Small lemon and lime bars that were a winner at just 5p. Could double up as a limescale remover, though much tastier.

3.

Refresher: Award-winning yellow chew filled with some powdery substance that even Tour de France riders of the late 1990s would have feared to take. At just 3p these had the 'sub-5p–more-than-2p' market covered until some CEO had the brainwave to challenge the 10p market and make the Refresher into a full-size bar. It was a disaster. Losing its 3p customer base and unable to compete with the 10p giants, the Refresher would never be the same again.

2.

Wham Bar: The godfather of the chew market. The chew bar that would make you an offer you couldn't refuse. That offer was the colour pinky-red (masquerading as raspberry) with green-purple crystals in it that were like a childhood version of injectable crack. The Wham Bar's Achilles heel was its wrapper, which was impossible to open without getting some of it stuck on the bar. Of all the chew bars, the Wham Bar was probably the only one we children knew was bad for us. The Wham Bar retired in the early 1990s following a string of legal suits and a failed run for government.

1.

Stinger: If ever there was going to be a bar to challenge the Wham Bar's dominance, it had to be the Stinger. It seemed to have more E's in it than all the other chew bars combined and it was huge. Green with red powdery stuff in the centre the Stinger bar could destroy your teeth for ages. It had a non-stick wrapper that, like Teflon, was a by-product of war. Children loved it and it kept dentists in jobs for years.

'THE ...'

One great quirk of how many in Ireland talk, particularly the older generation and quite a few of the younger too, is our tendency to put 'the' in front of anything. While most commonly heard when talking about a business or a brand, it can occur at any time. While this probably has something to do to our native language, it is a sure-fire way of spotting someone is from Ireland (that and their accent of course).

When it impossible to put 'the' in front of a word, the fall-back option is to put an 's' at the end.

EXAMPLES OF THIS INCLUDE:

— *'I was reading **the** Facebook.'*

— *'Are you going to Lidl**s**?'*

— *'I was checking **the** Google.'*

— *'I saw a television on sale in Tesco**s**.'*

— *'I saw it on **the** Twitter.'*

— *'So how is **the** family?'*

And in rare cases you can mix both:

— *'Are you going over to **the** boyfriend**s** so?'*

IRISH IMMIGRATION OFFICIALS

I'm sure they know exactly what they are doing. I'm sure their years of street-smarts ensure they can spot a fake passport a football field away. And I'm sure if you are on an FBI/Garda Most Wanted list, they'd have you in hand-cuffs in seconds.

Still, from where the arriving Irish person stands, Irish immigration officials (traditionally two Gardaí in their forties) look like the most laid-back entry officials in the world.

While you could also use the words 'lethargic', 'bored' or 'utterly disinterested', I prefer to see them as skilled task men who deftly move from one elbow to the other, glancing at your passport before using their index finger to wave you home, with the occasional '*howya*' if you're lucky.

TEA (ALSO PRONOUNCED TAE!)

Tea, or tae, is the chief social lubricant of the Irish race. While we may not have invented it, discovered it, or even perfected it, it is as important to the country as the colour green. If it were to disappear in the morning, a sense of social nudity would occur that would see half the country recede into themselves, uncertain as to how they should deal with a variety of social situations.

Such is the ubiquitous nature of the substance tea that it can be used for a plethora of social circumstances, none of which involve being thirsty:

- Unexpected visitor arrives over to the house – tea
- Expected visitor arrives over to the house – tea
- Come home from school crying because you fell and cut your knee in the yard – tea
- Come home from college crying because she dumped you – tea

- Awkward silence as your son reveals he is gay – tea

- Awkward silence as unexpected pregnancy news announced – tea

- Shocking news – tea

- Fantastic news – tea

- Break in television programme – tea

- Break in conversation – tea

That said, tea also goes exceptionally well with a nice slice of warm buttery toast, particularly during breaks in work.

Finally two points for visitors to Ireland to note are:

1. All of the following questions and statements are of course rhetorical: a) '*Who's for tea?*', b) '*You'll have a cup of tea?*', c) '*You'll stay for a cup of tea?*', d) '*I was just making a cup of tea*', e) '*Let me get the kettle on*' and f) '*Tae?*'. You are being asked if you want tea in much the same way a drowning man is asked if he'd like some oxygen. It is expected that you will have some.

2. Secondly, in a traditional Irish household under absolutely no circumstances should you ask for Camomile, Peppermint, English Breakfast, Earl Grey, etc. Tea is tea. If the host is doing their job correctly the tea will be 'wet' and that should be enough for you.

IRISH BARBECUES

INSTRUCTIONS FOR AN IRISH BARBECUE:

Prior to the day:

- Tell your friends you're having a barbecue, accidentally giving them the wrong date. This will allow them to double-book themselves.

- Realise your mistake and tell your friends the proper date, explaining it's no problem that they are now going to a landscaping festival in Sligo. You completely understand. Console yourself with not having to buy as many cocktail sausages as previously planned.

- Buy a disposable barbecue in a large supermarket. Base your purchase on which one is likely to:

  - Never be used again.
  - Burn the biggest patch of grass in your garden.

- Buy drink. As it will surely be a wash-out, you should at least bask in some unfounded optimism in the days leading up the barbecue by being 'cider-heavy' in your purchasing while also getting a few cooler bags, ice and two camping chairs on special offer.

- Run around on the evening before buying meat. This is not because you wanted to wait until the last minute to get the freshest cuts but because you genuinely forgot about it. Meat should include the following:

  - Cocktail sausages and artisan sausages (expensive ones) to be brought out at the height of the barbecue
  - Burgers and chicken wings
  - Three steaks, one of which you have already put your name on and hidden behind the aloe vera juice in the fridge.

On the day:

- Invite a female family member on the morning, hoping that they have made a salad and have some burger buns, both of which you forgot.

- Ask a male family member on the morning to see if they will give you a hand putting up a tarpaulin over the barbecue, because it is already raining heavily.

- Start up the barbecue.

- Stare at the barbecue wondering why it won't light properly. Opening a beverage may help (with the staring, not the starting).

- Look away as someone (your old house-mate from college) adds something ridiculously flammable to the barbecue, which, while nearly setting fire to both him and the tarpaulin, actually does the job.

- Pair up your best mates based on what they have in common: looking forward to the football season; cars; androgyny, etc., and allow them to take over the barbecue.

- Freeing yourself up, get another beverage and balance glancing at the football now on TV with looking at the weather, wondering if the rain is going to clear.

- It won't.

- Start bringing in the food, telling everyone to help themselves.

- They will.

- The barbecue will officially end when the following combination of factors intersect:

  - Everyone is full.

  - The partner not drinking whose turn it is to drive has had enough of their drunk other half and decides it is now time to leave.

  - The babysitters need to be relieved.

  - It's time to relocate to the pub.

  - The sun comes out.

'WHO SAiD MASS?'

You'll see them drifting along country roads between the early hours of 9am and midday. You'll see them sneak into their friend's place, whose parents are agnostic. And you'll see them having a sneaky 'puck around' at the local football field as the pitch gets marked out for the day's games.

You'll then see them check their watches, realise that 40 minutes are up and head for home and Sunday lunch. And then you'll see them try to ring their sister, brother or enquiring off someone wearing good shoes, asking them that age-old question, 'who said mass?'

As the years have progressed and with the advent of the live radio transmission of the local Sunday service, life has become a little bit easier for those who skip the occasional mass. All they now need to do is locate the right radio-wave, recognise the priest's voice and not overplay their hand when they come home by commenting on the Prodigal Son sermon when it's actually Palm Sunday.

CiDER

APPLES + TiME = CiDER

In Ireland we have a lot of apples.

In the evenings we have a lot of time.

It's hardly surprising then that cider is quickly becoming one of the more popular drinks in Ireland.

In Ireland you can drink cider in four distinct ways:

1. FROM A PiNT GLASS WiTH iCE: This will allow you to imagine that it is 26°C outside and you are in the outdoors with the warm summer sun falling down on you, even if it is January and you haven't seen a beer garden in more than four months.

2. FROM A PINT GLASS WITH NO ICE: With no space taken up with silly frozen water and no head on it, this lets you fit more cider in, thus allowing you to forget faster that you haven't seen a beer garden in more than four months.

3. FROM A CAN: This is a perfect accompaniment for music festivals, informal summer barbecues and sleeping rough.

4. FROM A BOTTLE: This final option should preferably be a bottle of artisan Irish craft cider produced somewhere in West Cork. Such a drink will help frame the perfect impression of you as someone who, yes, used to walk around music festivals completely sozzled with a half crumbled can of cheap cider looking for the shift, but now has a well-paid job and drinks craft cider because it doesn't affect your morning runs.

THATCHED COTTAGES

Cool in summer, warm in winter, thatched cottages used to be a common characteristic of country Ireland.

Unfortunately over the years thatched cottages became increasingly scarce. This was part due to previous government policies that encouraged cottagers to change their straw roofs for tin (possibly out of some bias stemming from *The Wizard of Oz*) and also due to the fact that the roofs had to be replaced once every decade, unless of course they burnt down in the meantime!

Thankfully there has been something of a renaissance in thatched cottages in recent times, which is great both for those living in these charming wonders and also for certain Irish postcard manufacturers who like to suggest that everyone in Ireland has one.

BiG FAMiLiES

While 2.4 is the required number of children needed to sustain a population, Ireland is not alone in Europe at lagging slightly behind the mark, with a current rate of 2.05.

Of course it wasn't always like this and not very long ago Ireland was bringing up the European average with ridiculously large families.

Due to a perfect storm of Catholicism, the prohibition of contraception, shit weather and worse TV, Irish families burgeoned with 10+ children an accepted norm both in the city and the countryside.

As a result of such large numbers, Irish families would be characterised for years by savage reunions (often involving legendary games of Tip the Can between offspring), lengthy Christmas card lists and wedding invitation nightmares.

JOHN 3:7

For years as children watching Gaelic games, when another point would sail over the bar towards the Hill 16, we would see a bright yellow and black sign appearing that read '*John 3:7*'. And we would wonder:

~ Is it the same person all the time?

~ Do they have to pay for tickets?

~ Are they watching the match as well?

~ Does it affect those standing behind them?

~ Is that something to do with the score?

~ And if it isn't the score, who the hell is John?!

It turned out not to be the amount scored by the Kilkenny hurlers or by the Dublin footballers in the final five minutes of the first half to bury another county's annual title ambitions but the work of a man called Frank Hogan. For more than two decades Frank brought the sign around with him from game to game to tell people (as long as they could understand scripture) that the Bible says:

'It's going high, high, high and drifting ... wide of the posts.'

Either that or maybe:

'Marvel not that I said unto thee, Ye must be born again.'

LUCK

'THE LUCK OF THE IRISH'

No other country in the world is perhaps more synonymous with luck than Ireland. Unfortunately, what they don't tell you is that the luck being referred to is generally bad luck, as any quick glance at Irish history will tell you.

Bad luck: Ireland breaks away from the landmass that is Europe only to look over our shoulders and realise that one of the world's most powerful colonial powers, Britain, has had the same idea.

Analysis: It wasn't like we could have asked the tectonic plates to send us elsewhere.

BAD LUCK-O-METER: 85%

Bad luck: Ireland relocates as an island nation in the middle of the North Atlantic prevailing wind, meaning that while we will have four seasons to the year, they will all be cold, wet and windy.

Analysis: Unless there was a form we forgot to fill out enti-tled 'preferred island location', we can hardly be held responsible for the earth's weather.

BAD LUCK-O-METER: 79%

Bad luck: Ireland experiences its first real foreign invasion in 1169 when the Normans arrive. Though they might sound like a middle-class family from upstate Idaho, they are in fact a well-armed, well-drilled, fighting force originating in Northern France who quickly take over.

Analysis: Only ourselves to blame for this one really, con-sidering we actually asked them over! That said, it wasn't actually a national invite but the idea of one man, resident villain Dermot MacMurrough.

BAD LUCK-O-METER: 65%

Bad luck: Ireland has so many failed rebellions, uprisings and revolutions that we start to get a 10% discount off them.

Analysis: To lose one rebellion is unlucky, two a little care-less, but a dozen really is taking the piss.

BAD LUCK-O-METER: 51%

Bad luck: Ireland relies solely on the one crop (the potato) for breakfast, lunch and dinner. The crop then fails and we starve in an event we call 'the Great Famine', even though it wasn't great at all!

Analysis: Due to the Penal Laws we weren't exactly in a position to open a 24-hour Centra to solve our hunger, and due to high levels of illiteracy a Jamie Oliver/Darina Allen-esque *30-Minute Meals for the Irish Peasant* cookbook would have been of little benefit. Perhaps we could have sewn a few more onions, carrots or given grass one more go.

BAD LUCK-O-METER: 80%

Bad luck: Ireland finally gets independence and has a Civil War to celebrate.

Analysis: What were we thinking?!

BAD LUCK-O-METER: 46%

FLASHING YOU THE LIGHTS

Maybe it is a hangover from colonial times but for some reason Irish people have a strange distrust of An Garda Síochána and, in particular, their traffic corps. One way this manifests itself is just how far the average Irish motorist will go to warn oncoming traffic that there is a police check-point up ahead or better yet, a speed camera.

In certain countries flashing your lights at an oncoming vehicle usually means:

A) YOU KNOW THEM

or

B) THERE IS AN ACCIDENT/DOWNED TREE/SOMEONE ON HORSEBACK AHEAD.

In Ireland however, if someone is uncontrollably flashing their lights at you, it can only mean one thing: a Gardaí Gatso speed van is around the corner. And it doesn't matter if you are a pensioner 3 km/h over the speed limit or al-Shabaab jihadists on the move, the Irish motorist has your back and will alert you all the same.

BACON
AND CABBAGE

Since the dawn of time, or shortly thereafter, there has been one meal that has dominated Irish dinner tables. While as a nation we may have dabbled with shepherd's pie, tried spaghetti Bolognese and even flirted with a bit of Thai green curry, it is bacon and cabbage that we always come back to.

Voted favourite Irish dinner a whopping 75 out of the last 87 years and never out of the top 3, bacon and cabbage occupies the same position of respect as Irish mothers, Guinness and sunny spells.

To slag off bacon and cabbage is just inviting trouble, so you just don't do it. And why would you? After all the meal is a culinary art-form and national delicacy, as the following recipe reveals:

RECiPE:

- Put a bacon joint in the pot and boil.

- Put a cabbage in the pot and boil.

- Remove the scum. (Anyone who has ever cooked bacon and cabbage knows what I mean.)

- *Voilà*!
  - If you want to go fancy, add white sauce (flour, butter, milk and a herb of some sort, usually parsley).
  - If you've got the cousins over, add root vegetables to bulk it up.

SERViNG SUGGESTiON:

On a plate with potatoes (preferably boiled).

LiGHTING
A CANDLE

Long before insurance policies took hold in Ireland, Irish mothers were responsible for guarding against injury, ill will or accident. They did this by lighting a candle.

Lighting a candle was a sure-fire way of warding off misfortune or inviting success:

> Irish mothers lit candles for when you were doing the driving test or sitting the Leaving Cert.

> They lit them from Lent to Christmas.

> They lit them for births, deaths and everything in between.

> They lit them if you had tooth-ache, head-ache or heart-ache.

> They lit them for those getting onto a plane or coming off one.

- They lit them for the job interview, the first day at work and that you'd get home safe from the office party.

- They lit them when you were getting your appendix out or a filling put in.

- They lit them for those heading to purgatory and for those on their way back.

- They lit them for everything.

Sometimes if it was really serious, like if you hadn't studied for your exams, they'd call in the grandmother to get her to light one too! In fact such was the importance of lighting the candle there was even a state-sponsored policy around it once when, for the eve of the new millennium, the government sent a candle to every house in the country. Irish mothers did the rest.

SALLY O'BRIEN (AND THE WAY SHE MIGHT LOOK AT YOU)

For years Sally O'Brien was the most desirable girl in Ireland. Sweet, shy and sexy, she was the girl of every Irish man's dreams, even though she was entirely fictitious.

Arriving into our lives during a Harp Lager advert in 1980, she came into both our living room and the bar, wandering through a crowd of friendly strangers only to hesitate and look across at you. At this point a smile broke out from below her dark curly brown fringe and across her red crimson lips. Of course you couldn't be sure if she was looking directly at you or over your shoulder at your friend, even if he wasn't in the sitting room with you. But it didn't matter because it was some smile.

It is a testament to her beauty that we remember the advert decades later for Sally O'Brien and not the man narrating it who recounts all the things he misses about Ireland like the rain, the greenness and the pint of Harp, something he mentions five feckin' times in the course of 43 seconds! This of course begs the question of whether he had a drink problem before or after he went out to the hot foreign climes in which he now works, where apparently it's perfectly acceptable to sit on a deck-chair writing letters home as the crew of YMCA move pipes beside you!

Sally herself would remain single for more than a year (or at least until the advert ran its course) before moving abroad to work as a waitress in southern France, taking the hearts of many an Irishman with her.

MATCH-MAKING FESTIVALS

(OKAY, MAYBE IT'S JUST THE ONE.)

For some people, slow sets and social media are simply not enough when it comes to finding love. Due to heavy work-loads, bad luck or lambing season, they have been unable to meet that special person and need a little help. Thankfully for would-be romantics, that help comes in the guise of one of Europe's largest match-making festivals help every September in Lisdoonvarna. Here under the careful gaze of Willie Daly, a fourth-generation match-maker, 40,000 hopefuls come looking for love.

During this month-long shindig, men, women and farmers from across Ireland, Europe and beyond arrive hoping to find their soul-mate or at the very least, someone with good teeth. However if you don't find the 'one' before October's slurry restrictions or a final harvest call you home, then at least there's the month-long revelry to make up for it.

'THE STATE OF ...'

In Ireland one common insult we like to roll out is to draw attention to '*the state of*' somebody or something, almost always preceded by '*look at*' to more purposefully underline the fact. The phrase is multi-functional and may be heard in the following scenarios:

◆ **'Look at the state of the place'**: This generally refers to either your kitchen and/or the sitting room and is sometimes heard when you return to your apartment to find out that your house-mate has widened his 'dishwashing strike' to include a boycott on putting cutlery in the sink. This statement is not to be mixed up with '*Look at the state of **this** place/room*', employed solely by disapproving mothers when referring to your bedroom and/or the bedsit you've been renting.

◆ **'Look at the state of yer wan'**: A familiar phrase overheard from women talking about another woman. The woman in question will usually have been painted with a skin-tan best described as 'Chernobyl Blossom', have heels so high that she would be the first one to go in a zombie attack, be wearing something that straddles the border between skirt and shirt for the length of it and will, under no circumstances, have in her possession a jacket of any sort, despite it being late November.

◆ *'**Look at the state of yer man**'*: Commonly used in night-clubs about a 30-year-old who, urged on by more than a half dozen pints of lager, is slowly staggering his way through every girl in the house asking them if they would be interested in a dance. They will all say no, including the pillar he mistakes for a tall brunette.

◆ *'**Look at the state of it!**'*: Often proceeded by '*Oh Jaysus!*' and perfect for when you:

— Look at your hair after a bit of home-haircutting prior to a night out.

— Reflect on the new go-fast stripes on your car that are the result of underestimating the closeness of a shopping-car-park pillar.

— Realise the cake is ruined because you spent the last half hour talking about yer wan' from last night.

◆ **'Look at the state of him'**: Exclusively used by mothers who have discovered that their 3-year-old son has worn his mass clothes to go out back to build an underground apartment for worms.

◆ **'Look at the state of you'**: Regularly used by a man or woman on collecting their other half from a Friday night out (that started in the afternoon) with work colleagues.

◆ Finally the other common usage is the more critically reflective **'I must have been in some state'**, which is used by individuals who:

— Can't remember being the one slowly staggering through a dance-floor of females.

— Can't understand why their other half is not talking to them this morning.

— Can't figure out how on earth one of their socks has made on to the roof of the local Londis.

GLENROE

When it came to saucy, it didn't come much saucier than when Miley Byrne began romping on a hay bale with Fidelma Kelly in the village of Glenroe back in 1997. It said a lot about the state of the country that at the time we were so scandalised that our man Miley would be carrying on with his wife's cousin that we were oblivious to the fact he was doing so with one of his ridiculous stripey brown jumpers on. But that was 'Glenroe' for you.

Nowadays we might accept extra-marital affairs as the bread and butter of your daily soap opera but back then all of this was new to the Irish television viewer, particularly those living in what was known as 'two-channel land'. What was not new was that 'Glenroe' had been a pace-setter of domestic television drama for many years at that stage and Irish people couldn't get enough of it. (Of course children hated it, partly due to what they perceived was its distinct lack of quality and partly because 'Glenroe' meant that the weekend was now officially over).

The show had been mixing it up for years, from when it first hit our screens back in 1983. We had everyone's favourite uncle Dinny Byrne tip milk into a stream, showing us that we all have the propensity towards evil; we had young children wanting to be the next Blackie Connors, traveller or no-traveller, so cool was he with his hat and devil-may-care attitude; there was Teasy McDaid throwing her eyelashes across the counter like a rabid middle-aged bartender; and of course parish priest Father Devereaux who ran off with a Protestant-Jewish woman!

It was mad stuff and many a Monday morning, Irish mothers across the land would ring Joe on the radio to vent their anger. Of course come the following Sunday, they'd sit down again with their cup of tea and be glued again to that small make-believe village in Wicklow.

'Glenroe' finished up in 2001 but sometimes, usually around half past eight on a Sunday evening, you might still catch a parent or grandparent now humming, '*do-do-do do do-do-do-do-doo do-do-do do do-do-do-doo, diddly-doo* …' as they slowly switch off from the latest reality TV crap and remember back fondly.

Glenroe
1983–2001
RIP
'Well holy God'

A BAD PiNT

On 22 November 1963 at 12.30pm in Dealey Plaza, Dallas, Texas, the 35th President of the United States John F. Kennedy was assassinated, dead! Lee Harvey Oswald, the main suspect, never lived to see the trial and many now believe that he was only a patsy in the whole shebang and that the true culprit was a 'bad pint'.

Nearly a hundred years earlier on 7 November 1872, the *Mary Celeste* departed New York with Captain Briggs, his family and a crew of eight aboard. Expected in Italy several weeks later it was found along the Straits of Gibraltar with all passengers now vanished yet everything else bar the logbook still intact. Some historians reckon that, believing the ship to be sinking during a localised squall, the captain had ordered all to abandon ship. Others now suspect it was a 'bad pint'.

In an area of water between Key West, Puerto Rico and Bermuda known as the Bermuda Triangle, multiple aircraft and ships have disappeared over the decades, never to be heard from again. Some people have pointed the finger at inclement weather, variations in electromagnetic activity, and methane gas bubbles. Others now blame a 'bad pint'.

And up until recently, the extinction of the dinosaurs caused much debate amongst the scientific community with meteorite showers, poisonous plants and climactic cooling considered possible culprits. Recent evidence however now points towards a 'bad pint'.

In fact there are very little unknowns left out there that cannot be explained by a 'bad pint'. This calamitous piece of misfortune had until recently been known to reside only in the Sunday and Monday bedrooms of Ireland when men and women woke up with severe morning-time migraines, churning stomachs and bouts of dizziness that could only be explained not by the dozen or so pints consumed the previous evening but by a 'bad pint'. Once looked into, it soon emerged that not only was this mystery 'bad pint' responsible for much of Ireland's absenteeism following weddings, funerals and county finals, it was also responsible for half the world's unsolved mysteries.

THE ROSE OF TRALEE

ESSENTiAL iNGREDiENTS FOR THE ROSE OF TRALEE:

♥ A man (the host) who reminds you of your very pleasant but terribly embarrassing Uncle Pat.

♥ A group of smiling young men (the escorts) who look like no one has told them yet that they will not be getting the shift from any of the girls they are chaperoning.

♥ A group of young women (the Roses) who all:

  — Have some tenuous link to Ireland.

  — Are beautiful – not that this contest is about appearance of course, honest.

  — Will either to dance, sing, play a musical instrument, recite a poem or spot-weld, in front of a live audience.

♥ A pale moon rising above a green mountain.

♥ And viewers at home who know exactly what they are getting into for two nights every year but who won't be able to draw themselves away until they see if their choice, usually the Southern Californian or '*yer wan from Darwin*', will win.

THIRTY-THREE

33: The phone prefix for France

33: The atomic number of arsenic

33: The bus route from Lower Abbey Street to Balbriggan

33: The hottest temperature ever recorded in Ireland

33: The smallest sum of two positive numbers, each of which is raised to the fifth power: $1^5 + 2^5 = 33$

33: The temperature at which water boils on the Newton Scale

33: The amount of vertebrae we have

33 AKA 'TURTY TREE': THE ACHILLES HEEL OF IRISH PRONUNCIATION

While the soft lilt of the Irish brogue helps lift us into the annual top 10 of most loved accents in the world, there is one word that slays us: 'thirty-three'. As if our school teachers never expected us to travel overseas, we as children were allowed to grow into adulthood without realising that we weren't able to count to a hundred without generating a smile amongst our foreign friends.

In fact so bad are we at the number that had Jesus been born in Ireland, we probably would have waited until he turned 34 before we crucified him, just so we could recount the story of his resurrection more easily.

BLACKBERRY PiCKiNG

For a short window of time every year, Irish men and women can return to an age before they knew how to sew, how to plough and how to use a self-service check-out at Tesco. They can become hunter-gatherers again and pull in along some by-road to harvest nature's natural bounty of blackberries. Indeed, along with the enjoyment that can be derived from living out your Bear Grylls-Mesolithic-rural Ireland fantasy, there are several others positives that this annual pursuit can provide:

◆ A saving of 25 cent on your weekly household bill when you add up the money saved by 'hunting' your own food minus the money spent on TCP and plasters after a few hours negotiating briers

◆ A great addition to autumnal pies, tarts and cakes

◆ A handy measure of Vitamin C

◆ Seasonally-coloured stool samples (subject to the amount you eat during picking)

◆ A nice family day out

◆ And a nostalgic dose of the only Seamus Heaney poem that you ever studied that didn't involve dying, death or drowned kittens

THE NATiONAL PLOUGHiNG CHAMPiONSHiPS

Take 200,000 people, the mud of Glastonbury, the family vibe of a Yellowstone picnic and the traffic of a London rush-hour. Then just add tractors and that will help give you a sense of Ireland's annual National Ploughing Championships.

Every year before schools really kick in and daylight really peters out, rural Ireland has one final opportunity to let it all go wild, down at the National Ploughing Championships. At it, farmers and farmerettes (yes, that's what they call them!) do battle as they drive tractors really slowly to plough the straightest, most well-cut, well-turned furrow.

Of course it is not just about the ploughing. It's also about the fun, the craic and the commotion, as well as discovering the latest in sheep feeds, trying to spot the Agricultural Minister, and getting into frame of a 'Nationwide' report. Good times.

DRIVING MILES FOR CHEAP DIESEL

Car takes approximately 63 litres of diesel.

Diesel costs 143.9 cent per litre at Fuel Station A, situated directly on the road home from work. A tank of diesel there costs €90.66.

Diesel costs 140.9 cent per litre at Fuel Station B, 5 miles and 25 minutes out of your way in a station run by some lads from Monaghan. This results in a tank of diesel costing €88.77.

Therefore you drive directly to Fuel Station B for a total saving of €1.89, which you then blow on a Galaxy Ripple and a packet of Monster Munch to keep you alert for the remaining drive back home.

You then proceed to tell everyone you know that the diesel is cheaper over in Fuel Station B in the same tone of voice as if you've just invented the cure for cancer.

KERRYGOLD (AND WHO TOOK THAT HORSE TO FRANCE)

To the uninitiated, Kerrygold is a block of butter, a knob of which goes well on freshly boiled potatoes, as a lively substitute for cooking oil or, if you are really stuck, leathered in between a few ham sandwiches.

To those in the know, Kerrygold is much more than that: it is an enigma, a cultural icon and the Dan Brown of dairy, behind one of Ireland's greatest mysteries, *'who's taking the horse to France?'*

Whether by accident or design, in the 1990s the advertising executives of Kerrygold had a brainwave. First they had to find some countryside, then a beautiful dapple-grey stallion, a Frenchwoman (identifiable both by her accent and her French haircut), an Irishman who looks like a mother-in-law's dream, a cheeky chappy who isn't afraid to ask the tough questions and finally an old woman whose face would sour milk and send boats back out to sea.

And when they found all these, they just needed to seemingly run out of funding halfway through the shoot and finish with the cheeky chappy asking, '*hey Dad, who's taking the horse to France?*' At this point the ad finished, with the man and woman looking into each other's eyes and thinking, '*what are the hell is this advert even about?*'

It was the television equivalent of the Bermuda Triangle. Ireland was agog. For days, weeks and even years people would occasionally wonder, sometimes waking up in the middle of the night thinking, '*who's taking the horse to France?*'

While there were many rumours about the dapple-grey stallion – that it never made it to France; that it found God and moved to Africa; that it started a new career as a burger; that it retired to play golf in the Algarve; or that it set itself on fire live on-stage in a small bar in downtown Detroit – it still remains a mystery and to this day Irish people don't know who did end up taking the horse to France.

FARMS

You don't have to go back very far to find a farm in everyone. Not in Ireland anyway. For those of us who grew up in
villages, towns and cities, there wasn't a greater adventure
than when we took off from behind the TV and went to visit
the uncles or aunts who still lived off the land.

There were great memories from these countryside excur-
sions:

- There were the bales of hay that made the greatest
  forts this side of the Maginot Line, from which you set
  up perimeters of defence with artillery full of conkers
  in the vain hope that the rest of the cousins would
  come down for an all-out mock war.

- There were the endless spare parts and metal pieces
  lying around that would have kept MacGyver going for
  years.

- There was the hunting and gathering where you
  headed down the fields to streams to fish out pin-
  keens and on boreen strolls for wild strawberries.

- There were the late-night drives home, huddled in the back of the car with stars shining, free from suburban lights.

- There were the collie-crosses and wee terriers who might bark hello but couldn't wait to jump up on your lap.

- There was the 'other yard', the one you didn't go near because it was dangerous and you wouldn't dare cross your uncle on that.

- There were the epic games of Tip the Can that lasted until dusk.

- There were the aunts and women of the house who prepared cauldrons of spuds, flavoured with butter, meat and gravy.

- And then there were your uncles who were heroes and legends, who might puck around with you and sometimes, very occasionally, would allow you to join them in their Massey Fergusons and John Deeres to see the world from where they sat.

NOT ASKING FOR SOMETHING

While this might sound terribly confusing to our foreign friends it really is quite simple: whenever an Irish person doesn't ask for something, there is a very good chance that they are actually asking for it.

For example, if at the dinner table someone wants the salt, they will not ask for it by saying, '*you **can't** pass me the salt there, can ya?*'

Or if they want to change the channel, you might hear them not ask, '*you're **not able** to throw me over the remote control, are ya?*'

Maybe it is due to a history of being let down or maybe it is some Irish language influence. Whatever the reason, in Ireland there is no better way to ask for something than by not asking for it.

'You'd **hardly** lend me your lawnmower, would ya?' means your garden is out of control and in need of a cutting.

'You **couldn't** spare us a few chips, could ya?' suggests you haven't had dinner yet.

'You **wouldn't** give me a lift to work in the morning, would ya?' of course informs us that your car is still in the garage.

While 'it's **not possible** that you'd give me your spare kidney, is it?' suggests that you're a little down the hospital waiting list.

However of all the questions that the Irish don't ask, probably our favourite is the one that has been bringing couples together for over a hundred years: 'There's **no chance** you'd think about going on a date with me, would ya?'

GAELIC FOOTBALL

Long diagonal balls, high fielding, diving blocks, mazy runs, points from the sideline, shots hard, high and into the roof of the net. When it is played right, in the right spirit, with the right adventure, Gaelic football is a joy to behold.

Players, who finish work after it's already dark, take to the club football pitch in the depths of winter to run the hard yards, hone their footwork and fight for places in the starting 15 come springtime. And amongst these, there will be some lucky ones who get to wear their county jersey and fight on an even greater stage. And amongst those lucky ones, there will be 30 luckier still who will find themselves on the greatest stage – Croke Park on the third Sunday of September. There they will play in front of family, friends, communities and county supporters who have managed to hunt tickets from every available source.

And there on this greatest stage, before this full house, in this special place, the ball will be thrown in and for the next 70 minutes and 2 minutes of added time, always 2 minutes of added time, they will fight for Sam.

THE BOOK OF KELLS

The Book of Kells is quite possibly the most decorative illumi-nated manuscript Gospel book ever made. Put a little more simply, it is the world's best coloured-in Bible.

While there remains some controversy over where exactly it was created, what is generally agreed is that sometime around the late 8th century, the best drawers, designers, doo-dlers and colourers from around Ireland and Britain came together and decided to give the Bible a 9th-century trans-formation. In what would become the Gok Wan of religious manuscript makeovers, traditional Christian iconography met with the ornate swirling motifs typical of Hiberno-Saxon art, all brought together on high-quality calf vellum.

It is quite remarkable that such a work of genius has remained with us for the last 1200 years, except for a short period of disappearance around 1007 when it was briefly stolen, only to turn up in the bedroom of a Travelodge a few months later. Since then it has been protected and passed through the ages to where it now proudly sits on display in Dublin's own Trinity College.

TRACTORS ON THE ROAD

Every year primarily between the months of June and September, a species of animal descends into Ireland like a flock of migratory birds and proceeds to take over the by-roads and back-roads of the country. That animal is the tractor.

There are several positives and negatives to this seasonal influx.

Negatives:

- They are impossible to overtake.

- Your confidence takes a blow when you see a 12-year-old driving a Massey Ferguson who you know is making more money an hour than you did until you were nearly 30.

- Leaves, twigs and small branches wash over your car as the tractor in front streams under and through low lying trees.

- They are impossible to overtake.

- In another blow to your confidence, you spot the 12-year-old's 16-year-old brother driving a combine harvester the size of your first home, which he probably bought from last summer's earnings.

- Their drivers are able to look over the hedgerows into the green and golden countryside, which partially explains their slowness.

- They are still impossible to overtake with a strict mathematical equation that says:

The number of minutes you are running late + the relative importance of the meeting you are driving to x the number of children you have to collect on your way home + the number of bales being carried = % chance you have meeting a tractor en route.

Positives:

- You know you are in Ireland, you know it is the summer and you know that if the tractors are out, there is a good chance that the sun is too.

THE 'JUST A MINUTE QUIZ'

There were several voices that people in Ireland grew up with that became so much part of your weekly life, they may as well have been your kin. Larry Gogan was one of those voices.

Larry was like your uncle except on the radio. He was easily as old as your real uncles but a good deal cooler with his depth of musical knowledge. What was coolest about Larry though was not his track choices but his legendary 'Just a Minute Quiz' that allowed the Irish public take a daily break for 60 seconds and test their general knowledge against the clock.

Though it was a simple idea it became the stuff of legend, so much so that a whole sub-culture grew up around the supposed questions and answers that had occurred over those 60 seconds:

Q. *'Name something a blind man might use.'*
A. *'A sword.'*

Q. *'What is the capital of France?'*
A. *'F.'*

Q. *'Where is the Taj Mahal?'*
A. *'Opposite the Dental Hospital.'*

Q. *'What was Hitler's first name?'*
A. *'Heil.'*

Q. *'Can you divide 48 by 16?'*
A. *'Yes.'*

Q. *'What would be doing if you were on the piste?'*
A. *'On the beer.'*

Q. *'Complete the saying "As happy as …"'* (at which point Larry gives a clue by telling the contestant to think of his name).
A. *'A pig in shit.'*

And no matter how badly you did, Larry, ever the gentleman, would be on hand to console the contestant with his ubiquitous *'they didn't really suit you'*.

THE AMOUNT OF WORDS WE HAVE FOR BEING DRUNK

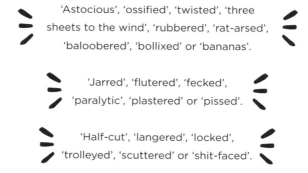

'Astocious', 'ossified', 'twisted', 'three sheets to the wind', 'rubbered', 'rat-arsed', 'baloobered', 'bollixed' or 'bananas'.

'Jarred', 'flutered', 'fecked', 'paralytic', 'plastered' or 'pissed'.

'Half-cut', 'langered', 'locked', 'trolleyed', 'scuttered' or 'shit-faced'.

The list of ways we Irish have to say the word 'drunk' seems to be endless.

Thankfully though, with the increased popularity of running and the advent of spin classes and online dating, the amount of times we now need to use these words has started to decrease.

Consequently, rather than seeing the number of Irish words for 'drunk' as a glorification of alcohol, we can now view them as evidence of our colourful use of language, particularly *as Gaeilge*, where we have even more colourful ways of saying it with:

- *'Ar meisce'* being the most common
- *'Ar stealladh na ngrást'*, for being drunk enough that you are in a state of pouring out compliments or grace
- *'Coach ar meisce'*, for being blind drunk
- *'Ar deargmeisce'*, for being really drunk
- *'Gan féith ná comhaireamh a bheith agat'*, for being so dead drunk that, almost quite literally, you are without a sign of life

And our two favourites:

- *'Bhí an hata ar leath cheann aige'*, for when your hat is literally halfway down your head.
- *'Bhí dhá thaobh dan bhóthar aige'*, for when you are literally 'both sides of the road'!

MASS

LEARNINGS FROM AN IRISH MASS:

~ At least one person will forget their seat after communion.

~ While you will get used to and eventually enjoy the taste of unleavened bread, you're fecked if it sticks to the top of your mouth.

~ The missionaries home from Africa give the best sermons.

~ Leaving mass at communion is like leaving Croke Park before the final whistle – it's only acceptable in certain circumstances.

~ You're four times as likely to be seated behind a man who sneezes into his hand than the girl next door, something you only remember when you're all asked to shake hands.

~ On the one time the girl next door sits in front of you, you will not have a penny for the collection box and she'll notice.

~ You will never, ever fully nail the genuflection. Get over it.

~ Priests aren't great at punch-lines and parishioners aren't a tough crowd.

~ The front rows are dominated by newly-weds, newly-parents and nuns.

~ You know you've made it the first day you do the collection baskets.

~ Just because you know the Nicene Creed off by heart doesn't guarantee you'll do well in the Junior Cert.

~ The whole thing with the rich man into heaven was a misunderstanding. He just had to work harder, that's all.

~ There's nothing really on television anyway this time on a Sunday morning.

~ Under 40 minutes is fine; under a half hour is a God-send.

SET-DANCING

To the untrained eye, Irish set-dancing might look like a violent mating ritual for a room full of swingers. And it's easy to understand why: multiple partners, wild human orbits and dances with names such as 'Labasheeda', 'Spa Televara' and 'the Portmagee Miserk'. However it is important to look beyond this and if ever the opportunity presents itself to get involved, you should just jump in.

If that occasion ever does arise, a few tips:

- Don't just jump in. That's how injuries happen.

- If you want to take part, stand close to the action smiling and looking curious. A grandmother who looks the other side of 80 will soon pull you in. Wearing anything that might make people believe you are from the US also works.

- If in doubt, follow the direction of the jocular and slightly heavy-set aunt.

- If you have just downed three bourbons at the bar to celebrate someone's birthday, perhaps this is not the time to try the Ballyvourney Reel.

- Under no circumstances should you attempt to chat someone up while dancing. You will lose concentration and rear-end a granny. Not cool.

- Beware the overly energetic country uncle full of stout. Tell-tale signs include hairy hands, Guinness marks down his shirt and being suddenly propelled across a table full of drinks.

- Wait until at least the third set before you starting shouting '*Yeeooowwww!*'

- Turns with two men in a row means that you've fecked up badly. Look for the jocular aunt to set you right.

- Finally, when the music stops, clap, smile and feel free to turn to the person beside you and say something like '*Jaysus, that's powerful stuff that*'. At this point you may now approach the girl who caught your eye but only do so when you can see just one of her and the room has ceased spinning.

WAVING TO STRANGERS WHILE DRIVING

INSTRUCTIONS FOR WAVING TO STRANGERS WHILE DRIVING:

1. Do not worry that you don't know them. They don't know you either. At best you might remind them of a niece or nephew who has immigrated to Australia.

2. Waving should only be done in the countryside. Waving to strangers in towns is just plain weird.

3. Never take your hand off the wheel when waving. This is not a safety issue but rather because if you do, you'll either make the person:

- Feel bad that they didn't recognise you, because only an 'eejit' would wave like that unless they genuinely knew you
- Think you're a 'eejit'.

4. Waving should be a short, sharp raise of four fingers that will either elicit the same response or a nod of the head. Nods of the head are cooler.

5. Do not substitute flashing your lights at an oncoming car for a wave. This will simply scare them into thinking that:

- Cattle are crossing, someone is on horseback or a labrador is wandering free, all of which will slow them down to a crawl for the next 10 minutes.
- The Gardaí are around the corner, which, because their tax is out, will force them to turn around.
- Something on their car isn't working, which will make them pull over to check their tyres.

6. Don't be surprised if you start to feel good about yourself. Strangers waving at you has that effect – just ask the Queen.

7. Under no circumstances should you take a high proportion of a village waving at you as an invitation to up sticks and relocate to the countryside.

8. And don't be surprised if very few people wave back at you. This can occasionally happen for a number of reasons:

- The community's local Junior B hurlers lost last weekend and are now out of the Championship.
- The community you're driving through has had a boil notice in effect for the last decade.
- You have a Dublin license plate.

IRiSH SKiN

THE IRiSH SKiN iS TO SUN AS ...

... alcohol is to safe driving.

... stalking is to romance.

... running 10k is to sleep.

... breaking mirrors is to music.

... heroin is to healthy living.

... leaving children in a parked car while you go window-shopping is to good parenting.

But as a way of identifying a fellow countryman or woman in a bus-load of strangers, aside from bad teeth and them wearing their county jersey, the Irish skin – pasty, salmon-like, refuses to tan in any sort of uniform fashion – has few equals.

THE ODD FLUTTER

ODDS ON, EVEN MONEY, 6/4, JOINT FAVOURITE, WORTH A FLUTTER, 15/2, EACH WAY, STARTING TO DRIFT, FRIENDLESS IN THE MARKET, 33/1, STILL RUNNING.

There is something in the Irish blood that seems to love 'the odd flutter', particularly on the horses. For most this is usually on:

∽ The Aintree Grand National, when everyone at work picks a horse in a sweepstake 35+ horse lottery. Of course you will always end up with the 150/1 longshot called 'Just a Nag', 'Losing Ground' or 'Knuckled on Landing' whose name you'll only hear when they unseat their rider at the second

∽ Cheltenham, when productivity levels around the office dip dramatically between the hours of 1.30pm and 4.45pm for a week in mid-March.

However there is one other time the Irish love the odd flutter: when they come across a 'tip'.

There are two things you should know about a tip. Firstly, the more circuitous the way you come across the tip, the more certain you can be that it will win. (It won't of course, but this should not affect your certainty.) Secondly, to decide on the amount of money you should put on this tip, you need to answer the following questions about the person you got the tip off and about where the horse will race:

- ❧ Were they wearing mucky boots of some description?

- ❧ Were they wearing one of those green wax jackets?

- ❧ Were they small enough to fit on a horse?

- ❧ Were they a stranger?

- ❧ Were they cutting your hair at the time?

- ❧ Did you accidentally overhear them give or get the tip over the phone?

- ❧ Is it on a racecourse that you never knew even existed?

- ❧ Is it a handicap race somewhere down the country?

- ❧ Do you feel lucky?

- ❧ Can the electricity bill wait until Monday?

If the answer to the majority of these questions is a 'yes', then you have no other option left but to put the money on it.

MiD-WEEK TRAiNiNG

Before the warmth of spin classes and the growth of running, the only real exercise opportunities open to the Irish male and female were the mid-week training sessions down at the local GAA pitch.

While these might occasionally occur in beautiful evening autumnal sunshine, more often than not they happened on wet wintry nights and the only thought that could keep you going was your dream of a final come summer.

Other characteristics of these trainings were:

- Losing three footballs over the nets before you've begun a lap

- A stinger across the legs before you've even warmed up

- Loads of running, though all with the ball

- Lads coming out of the woodwork on the eve of a Junior B hurling final

- The ubiquitous backs vs forwards debate

- Showers still not working or what was worse ...

- Showers not being turned on

BLESSING THE CAR

> Prolonged debate with the garage before kicking the tyres and agreeing to buy the car for €450 less than the asking prize: **€3,200**

> Car tax for the quarter: **€115**

> Annual insurance with some internet company whose excess is worth more than the car but whose advert made you laugh: **€672**

> Tank filled with petrol (not diesel, which you discovered when the nozzle didn't fit): **€65**

> Beaded seat covers that supposedly help alleviate back-ache on long journeys bought as a present by your younger brother (that you will never use because you are not a New York taxi driver from the Maghreb): **€22**

> Steering lock bought by your father that's made from an '–inium' you've never heard of: **€18**

> Air-freshener that's called 'vanilla dawn', 'wet pine' or 'burnt clutch' for that new car feel: **€2**

> Bringing the car to a parish priest so he can bless it and all who travel with it: **Priceless**

While most of us might put our confidence in our seat-belts, ABS brakes, air-bags and insurance policies, there is a small portion of the Irish population that will continue to put its faith in the patron saint of motorists, St Joseph. For as the saying goes, *'while there are some car safety things that money can buy, for everything else there's holy water'*.

IRELAND'S 'OTHER CRISPS'

For a country that was never known for its culinary variety, Ireland always punched well above its weight when it came to creating nutritionally poor alternatives to the regular potato crisp, aka 'other crisps'. They enjoyed a period of dominance at the end of the 1980s, and while they may have been a dietician's worst nightmare, these 10p staples were often the only thing that kept school-children going as they waded through corned beef and banana sandwiches.

THESE WERE SOME OF OUR FAVOURITES:

♥ **Chipsticks:** These were the original lick-your-fingers crisp. You could also entertain yourself with Chipsticks by sticking them in between your fingers or pretending to smoke them (something that was probably only marginally less healthy for you than they were).

♥ **Wagon Wheels:** It was easy to spot the children who would grow up and start a pension before they turned 30 eating these. They were the ones who always left a complete wagon wheel to finish, none of the broken crap that ended up at the bottom of the packet.

♥ **Burger Bites:** 'Beef'-flavoured corn crisps that tasted nothing like beef, corn or indeed a burger. Every class had one student who could fit a whole packet of these into his mouth. Boys openly envied him while girls secretly adored him.

♥ **Cheesepuffs:** Puff crisps that tasted of cheese. A double-edged sword really. On the one hand, you were rarely asked to share. But that was because so few people would go near you, so strong was the stench coming from the packet.

♥ **Skips:** Prawn cocktail-flavoured. What did that even mean? The best thing about these was that they fizzled on your tongue like a funky communion wafer. Skips cornered the prawn cocktail market until the arrival of Prawn Cocktail Crunchies, something that caused a bloody turf war in several parts of Offaly.

♥ **Snax:** Like Skips but not.

♥ **Onion Rings:** A date killer through and through. While strangely tasty, onion rings had the unfortunate reputation, along with Lion Bars and Canadian Dry, as the only thing left in your man's confectionary hut on match day Sundays.

♥ **Meanies:** Pickled onion-flavoured. Meanies were proper 'other crisps', with just the right amount of crunch, spirit, taste, tang and smell. Unfortunately the success went to their head and they went the way of the Refresher bar and sold out to become Mega Meanies, distancing their loyal fan-base. Things went down-hill from there and they've been checking in and out of the Betty Ford Clinic ever since.

♥ **Chickatees:** These were like a 'chicken'-flavoured Cheesepuff, except people would still sit beside you if you opened a bag.

♥ **Mummies:** Screaming green flavour that had a die-hard following out West. They would go the same way as CFCs and were taken off the market once a connection between them and depleting ozone layer was made.

♥ **Rancheros:** The smell from these 'bacon'-flavoured delights was so overpowering it is believed to be responsible for the great Roscommon classroom crisp ban from 1984 to 1986.

♥ **Other 'other crisps':** These were the flash in the pan 'other crisps' that captured the zeitgeist of the day and that may or may not have even existed outside an 8-year-old's consciousness. In the mid-1980s they included such noteworthies as **Barry McGuigan's** nettle-flavoured crisps and the **A-Team** collection of snacks.

♥ **Wheelies:** Rancheros with a combustible engine and a catalytic convertor for the smell.

♥ **Quavers:** These crisps were members of a family of snack movements collectively known as the Religious Society of Snacks. Quavers actively tried to avoid creeds and hierarchical structures between crisps.

♥ **Banshee Bones:** Which, if taken literally, would lead any budding student of the supernatural to believe that banshees suffered from rickets and smelt faintly of vinegar.

And then finally there was...

♥ **Monster Munch:** Monster Munch were a trail-blazer in the 'other crisp' market, being the first one to break the 10p transfer record, which some would say was to the eternal detriment of other snacks. Monster Munch were a 'beef'-flavoured full frontal crisp that was marketed around a whole list of mythological monsters. Of course the only monster ever to be found on the back of them was the cyclops, although it was rumoured that some village in East Cork had the entire series and that someone's cousin's friend had spotted someone eating a packet with a minotaur on the back of it.

BARMBRACK

BARMBRACK BY NUMBERS

214:
The combined amount of raisins and sultanas that go into a 'good' barmbrack

76:
The average age of those who consider a piece of barmbrack with a slice of butter to be amongst their top three foods

8:
The maximum amount of slices you can cut without risking exposing the ring inside

90%:
The chance that the ring is already exposed if you look at the bottom of the barmbrack

6:
The amount of people alive who can still remember the time barmbracks used to contain such things as a

pea – the person would not marry that year; a stick –
to symbolise an unhappy marriage; and a cloth –
to symbolise bad luck or poverty!

1:

The amount of slices needed to make you realise
that you don't really like barmbrack

364:

The amount of days required for you to forget that
you don't really like barmbrack before asking for
another slice, next Hallowe'en

85%:

The percentage chance your older sister has over you
in finding the ring ahead of you, giving rise to
theories your parents had it fixed

0.000002:

The cost per unit in cents of the ring in the barmbrack

3%:

The chance that finding the ring actually means you will
meet someone happily ever after the following year

THE FiELDS
OF ATHENRY

Written about a time before discount multiples, social welfare and JobBridge, 'The Fields of Athenry' tells the story of Michael, who, having fallen on hard times, possibly due to the construction slow-down, gets caught robbing '*Trevelyan's corn / so the young might see the morn*' and now is on a prison ship that '*lies waiting in the bay*'.

Had it occurred a hundred-odd years later, Michael would have gotten a suspended sentence, meaning that Mary would not now have to raise their '*child with dignity*' on her own.

Of course had Michael escaped with just a bit of community service, then Munster and Connacht rugby supporters, as well as all other Irish sporting fans, would have one less sporting anthem to roar out overseas to leave the hairs well and truly up on the back of your neck.

Altogether now ...

'LOWWWW LiE THE FiELDS OF ATHENRYYYY'

HALLOWE'EN

Though now a global phenomenon, a little known fact is that Hallowe'en has its origins firmly in the Gaelic Irish and Scottish festival of Samhain when the end of the harvest season was celebrated, the souls of the dead remembered and the darker side of the year began. Over time it would evolve and become what is today known world-wide as Hallowe'en.

While Hallowe'en now takes on various forms depending on what part of the world you live in, in Ireland some common characteristics that don't involve animal cruelty, losing your fingers or egging cyclists include:

⚡ **Trick-or-treating:** This is where you dress up as a witch or a ghost and a) call around your local housing estate during daylight hours because it is safer, or b) call up to the two neighbours in your country cul-de-sac lane, one of whom won't be about and the other having nothing more than a slice of barmbrack and a handful of monkey-nuts for you.

⚡ Dunking for apples game: A game in which those with fiercely prominent buck-teeth always clean up. This sometimes involves money.

⚡ Hanging apples game: Another fun activity that again seems part of a greater strategy to ration food in the house. Unless you can gently caress the Jonagold apple hanging off a nail from the doorway onto your shoulder, lull it into a false sense of security before attempting to maul it, the game is almost impossible to master. Often the only way you can succeed is by working together with someone else, usually a sibling, so that you simultaneously bite down on the apple. Wrong on many levels.

⚡ The flour game: A pyramid of flour with a small grape sitting atop. Participants have to slowly cut away segments of the flour, hoping the grape stays put. It is effectively a flour form of Jenga with no winners, only losers. A big favourite for little children, many of whom just want to dunk their heads in the flour anyway.

⚡ Lanterns: Also known as Jack-o-lanterns, carving these out has only increased in popularity since we started using pumpkins in Ireland instead of turnips.

- ⚡ **Bonfire:** This occurs in the back of your garden, using the hedge-cuttings your Dad has collected over the last month. Unfortunately due to the October damp, more often than not they generally fail to catch fire properly. This isn't a problem in housing estates however, as there is always an extra from a fire-safety video on hand with a tyre and a can of petrol just in case.

- ⚡ **Ghost story-telling:** Something that is always fun, until your older cousin veers off local ghost stories to give everyone a summary version of Stephen King's *It*.

- ⚡ **Fireworks:** The finale to the evening when your uncle sets off a dozen or so fireworks, bought in the border counties, whose quality is determined by the amount of Chinese written on them.

RiVAL SUPPORTERS SiTTiNG TOGETHER

Grown men will cry and shout and bawl and call the referee every name under the given sun. Grown women will be seen to do worse. When the blood gets up on Championship Sundays, almost anything can happen. But one thing that generally will not is the supporters going at each other.

It is a strange and satisfying fact of Irish sport that fans of rival county teams are allowed to sit and stand wherever they like.

On Championship Sundays you will not see rows of seats vacated and a line of fluorescent yellow separating the fans from Tipp and Kilkenny in the cauldron of Semple Stadium. There will no division between the big men from Tyrone and the not so wee men from Down in the beating drum of Clones. And even on 'the Hill', in an almost universal sea of blue when the Dubs are back home, you need not be alarmed if there is a small drop of green and yellow Royals or some Lilywhites amongst the Capital's Army.

Maybe it is because the game moves so fast and the score-board keeps ticking that there is only time to watch. Or maybe it is because we are such a small island that these rivals are our uncles and aunts, our wives and husbands and our work-mates and we will be chatting to them again tomorrow. Or maybe it is because Irish fans just don't do hooliganism in the much the same way they don't do Marmite.

And it is for this reason that inside our stadiums, you will see stands that are multi-coloured with fans from both sides chatting together, comparing their journeys down while sharing wine gums and the match day programme. Then there will be 70-odd minutes of roars for scores, curses for the ref and groans for balls and sliothars that go high, high but left and wide. And then when it's all over, a *'safe travel home'* will be cast along with either a *'well done'*, *'hard luck'* or *'see you again next week'*.

GOING TO CONFESSION

Visiting the doctor, having the car serviced, getting the teeth cleaned and clearing the gutters. These are several activities that form part and parcel of the Irish year. Going to confession is another.

At least once every twelve months, usually around Easter, the Irish mother comes in, turns off the television halfway through *Ben Hur* and sends you off to the church to confess.

While easy on paper (go in – confess – say a few prayers – gain absolution), confessions are a bewildering exercise for a teenage child. The reason for this is the confessional box, a place that defies the laws of physics.

◆ **Time:** While outside the confessional people seem to come and go with relative speed, once inside the confessional box, time seems to slow down, with days often passing before sight or sound of a priest.

◆ **Space:** Though the confessional box is so small that you have to reverse in, once the door closes behind you and light disappears it becomes immense. Disorientation quickly sets in and by the time the priest slides back the grille, you are either facing the wrong way or kneeling on the arm rest.

◆ **Sound:** Finally no matter how hard you try to listen, you can never hear what is being said in the neighbouring confessional less than two feet away, leading you to reasonably conclude that the confessional box were made of some God-like substance or possibly even lead.

Of course when the priest finally arrives, you are so relieved to be taken out of the darkness that you'd happily confess to anything with '*not helping at home*', '*kicking the sister*', '*pushing your younger brother*' and saying '*a few curses*' being the favourites. Occasionally the priest will cotton on to something a little greater and keep '*go on*'-ing you until you finally cave and admit to dropping the ladder on your older brother's new car and passing the blame onto the local car-wash. Then when the time is right the priest will finish with an '*okay then*' give you three Hail Marys and an Our Father, help you through the act of contrition and then absolve you of your sins.

WHISKEY

While the Scottish may like to claim a spiritual ownership of whiskey, Ireland too can look with pride at our long, glorious though occasional bleary-eyed relationship with the drink that in Irish we call 'uisce bheatha', meaning 'water of life'.

Jameson, Tullamore Dew, Tyrconnel, Kibeggan, Paddy, Bushmills, Red Breast and Powers are just some of the many Irish whiskeys that can be found around the land, with a host of craft whiskeys also beginning to emerge. More than the types of whiskey, however, are the types of people who drink whiskey, and it is easy to identify the type of person you are by the way you drink yours:

WHISKEY...

... WITH LEMON
You enjoy the little luxuries of life, hence your choice of Club Lemon as an accompaniment. You also like to listen to the harp during dinner and bring a hot-water bottle to bed.

... ON THE ROCKS

You wish it was still the '80s. Your ideal job is one where you could close deals or fire people over the phone as you cradle the receiver against your shoulder, with one hand on a putter and the other holding a whiskey on the rocks brought in by a secretary called Cindy. You are currently between jobs.

... WITH ICE

Isn't this the same as 'whiskey on the rocks'? Yes it is, but you would never dream of calling it this. As a result you have a stable income, a loving family and have a fine taste in European cinema. You pay into a pension plan, have a car from Sweden, buy fair trade tea and know what quinoa is. You have a dog who loves you, know how to change an oil filter, have never forgotten an anniversary and were a best man for five weddings before you turned 21. Bastard!

... AS A CHASER

You tell family you do not have a drink problem.
You tell friends you do not have a drink problem.
You tell strangers beside you, you do not have a drink problem.
You have a drink problem.

... WITH RED

You favourite football club is Celtic and you get angry if not everyone stands when the National Anthem comes on at the end of the night. You like the fact that this drinks sets you apart from every other country not because it is a more sophisticated but because no one outside Ireland knows what the 'red' actually means.

... NEAT

When not drinking your whiskey neat, you are probably starring in movies, planning your next heist or writing a script. You like to frequent unfamiliar bars wearing a suit without a tie. People think they know you but are too afraid to ask. There is a good chance you once shot a man in a duel.

... OUT OF A BOTTLE

If you drink it this way and are reading this book, you are either in the library solely to keep warm, this book is stolen or you are a multi-award-winning musician.

... STRAIGHT (DOWNED IN ONE GO)

You have either just experienced a shock and need to calm your nerves or will shortly be experiencing one when you wake up tomorrow morning, wondering why you are wearing a shirt and tie but naked from the waist down, and what on earth possessed you to put photos of someone else's family up on your sitting room wall? Holy crap, that's not your sitting room wall!

... WITH WATER

You are probably at least 80 and can remember the war. You can be found in the pub around lunch-time with the dog loyally beside you. You're warmly loved and regarded by friends and family, both living and dead.

... SOUR

Drinking whiskey this way suggests that you or forefathers at one stage owned slaves, ran a cotton plantation or are from Drumshambo. A drink as common in Ireland as a winter sandstorm.

... WITH COKE

You're either looking forward to your 21st birthday or have no shame. Excusing yourself because it just tastes so good is not an excuse.*

*You're right though – it does taste really good with Coke!

TIP THE CAN

Children across the world are experts in turning the most humdrum summer days into an adventure and a game. Perhaps the most universal of these from California to Cairo, Cartagena to Cork is that of 'chase', with Ireland's most popular variant of this being Tip the Can.

The rules are simple: the child who is on is known as 'it'. 'The can' in question changes from location to location and varies from gate-post and telegraph pole to elder tree and ESB box. 'It' has to stand at 'the can' and count to 20 with their eyes closed, no peeking. During this time everyone else runs for cover; hiding behind cars (foolish if they can't also raise their feet); stooping behind bushes (much more effective except during winter); hunching behind walls (solid); and for the high-risk and lazier, directly behind 'the can' hoping 'it' will take off their hand as soon as they finish counting so the hider can buzz in for safety.

Once the time is up, 'it' hunts down those hiding and, on spotting an ankle, an elbow or a dopey peek over a bunch of flowers, races back to 'the can' to declare '*tip the can, 1, 2, 3, I see Johnny behind the roses*'.

At this stage Johnny joins all the others in 'jail' whose hiding places have also been discovered. This continues until everyone is caught, with the first caught soon to become 'it' unless the last person standing, often your older sister, could stay silent as 'it' passes her hiding place and then manage to jump out of the tree, not sprain her ankle and get home first and shout '*tip the can, 1, 2, 3, I free everyone*', something older sisters are surprisingly good at until they go to secondary school and start liking boys.

PRAYING TO ST ANTHONY

'In 1222, a crack commando was sent to prison by a military court for a crime he didn't commit. This man promptly escaped from a maximum-security stockade to the Los Angeles underground. Today, still wanted by the government, he survives as a soldier of fortune. If you have lost something ... if no one else can find it ... and if you have a mother who has a statue of him ... maybe you can hire ... St Anthony.'

While St Anthony was never actually a member of the A-Team, his services were just as highly valued throughout Irish households. If you lost something that you couldn't find, even after you checked your room twice and retraced your steps just as you were told, then only one man could help: St Anthony.

With a small petition or prayer, 9 times out of 10, the lost item would eventually show up in either the most unlikeliest place like beside the carpet, under the gate, on eBay or in your pocket – *'but Mam, when I checked earlier it wasn't there!'* All thanks to St Anthony.

SAUSAGES

Sausages: even the name sounds tasty. In fact the name probably came before the food. There were probably hundreds of auditions for the part, all different types of food that wanted to be called a sausage, but in the end it went to a bundle of pig stuff. It was a worthy winner.

They have other sausages in other countries but in Ireland ours are special, as any good emigrant who has had to explain to customs what these pink things in their luggage are will tell you. The reason they taste so good is that our sausages have just the right amount of pork, fat and other stuff that makes them the ideal complement to a for Sunday breakfast, a toasted sandwich and high cholesterol.

EMiGRATiON

Every couple of decades, like the sudden movement of tectonic plates or a solar eclipse, a distinctive phenomenon takes place in Ireland as a generation of young people leave the island in another wave of emigration.

Unfortunately for the country, it is of course usually the wrong 100,000 who end up getting the boat overseas, leaving behind the men and women whose decisions were the reason they had to go in the first place. While such departures inevitably bring tears and heart-ache for family and friends as they bid goodbye to their loved ones, there are some positives:

- There is a huge jump forward in the technological advancement of parents and grandparents as they quickly master the telegram/the telephone/the internet/the Skype/the Snapchat.
- Particularly true in the 1980s, young Irish people realise there is more to life than blue jeans and permed hair.

- Our national consciousness increases as we look further outwards and realise that life and death doesn't begin and end at Sunday mass.

- Bedrooms quieten significantly as younger siblings get to choose whichever bunk-bed they like.

- The quality of Christmas presents increases dramatically.

- New opportunities for cheap holiday accommodation Down Under arise.

- Someone in the family finally gets a proper tan.

- Money is sent home, which helps to pay off that outstanding Credit Union loan on the Corolla.

- Men who haven't kicked a ball in almost a decade are brought out of retirement as spaces open up in the Junior C football as younger players head southwards.

- Ireland's reputation as a hard-working, hard-drinking, hard-to-understand nation spreads globally.

That said, we'd give it all back to have our brothers, sisters, cousins and friends home again.

LEAVING ON THE iMMERSiON

Things that scare the bejaysus out of Irish people (or at least used to) on a scale of 1–10:

Running out of tea when visitors come **—1.**

Nostradamus **—2.**

Dentists **—3.**

The dark **—4.**

Spiders **—5.**

Falling into a grave **—6.**

The Boogie Man **—7.**

Death **—8.**

Nuclear holocaust and/or Al Qaeda **—9.**

Leaving on the immersion* **—10.**

* The immersion: a water-heater that needs to be turned on in order to have a hot shower and that receives the same level of deference as a medium-level Hindu deity. Forgetting to turn off the immersion before going away for the weekend is a crime very few children come back from.

IRiSH CURSES

Ireland seems to be blessed when it comes to curses. Over time they have developed to be much more than insults or exclamations and now occupy a special place in the Irish heart.

There are effectively two types of curse.

The first type of curse is the singular ones, otherwise known as the '*shit, shite, bollix, bastard, feck and fuck*' range of curses. While there are many more, these curses act as substitutes for everything from adjectives to adverbs, prepositions to pronouns and are the most common form of curses used today. While not 'proper' English, the Irish public still warm to these and smile when we hear a breakfast DJ apologise after mistakenly playing the expletive-filled version of a new chart-topper or a sports commentator make excuses for a winning captain who starts off his interview with '*Fuck me! I can't believe it Marty!*'

The other type of curse is the traditional ones, the ones to be used against others. While versions of the above can be used here too, the more colourful ones are from our rich past and mean so much more, such as:

- ⚡ *'May you be afflicted with an itch but not have the nails to scratch it.'*

- ⚡ *'May your wood always be knotted.'*

- ⚡ *'May your children promise much but offer nothing.'*

- ⚡ *'May your kettle never boil.'*

- ⚡ *'May you find bees but no honey.'*

- ⚡ *'May your milk never churn.'*

- ⚡ *'May you always be a widow.'*

- ⚡ *'May you melt off the earth like snow off a ditch.'*

- ⚡ *'May you get the runs on your wedding night.'*

- ⚡ *'May the cat eat you and may the divil eat the cat.'*

And for when you have a little bit more time on your hands:

- ⚡ *'May those who love us love us.*
  And those that don't love us,
  May God turn their hearts.
  And if He doesn't turn their hearts,
  May he turn their ankles,
  So we'll know them by their limping.'

MAMS CUTTING HAIR

Letter-writing, footing turf and getting off the couch to turn the channel …

All lost arts that have become increasingly redundant in modern life. One other talent that has also gone the way of the dodo is the way Irish mothers used to cut your hair. For those who do remember this fading art, there were five distinct parts to this skill.

1. THE 'LEAN BACK AND LET ME WASH YOUR HAIR' PART: While this could be accomplished by the child simply bending over the bath tub, it was best achieved by the child leaning back into the sink. This way the maximum amount of both water and shampoo ('Clinic' preferably) could be splashed onto the floor and into the eyes.

Associated saying: '*It's only a bit of shampoo, it won't kill you!*'

2. THE DRYING THE HAIR PART: Only teenager daughters who did well in exams got to use the hairdryer and thus escaped this part. The rest of us were subject to a towel and an assault, as mothers took advantage of your blindness from the shampoo and the towel to knock the crap out of you, more so if you had recently got a bad note home from school.

Associated saying: *'If you stop moving about, it wouldn't hurt so much.'*

3. THE COMBING PART: The key to this was not to break early. If mothers sensed that you were in pain they would extend the combing for anything up to an hour. (My friend saw it done to his brother once.)

Associated saying: *'Sure, I'm going as slow as I can!'*

4. THE ACTUAL HAIRCUTTING PART: Using just their fingers for measurement and a scissors that hovered over your ears for fun, mothers moved from one side to the other like a wildfire spreading west, chopping away unnecessary hair until your head attained the same type of uniformity as 1960s socialist Russia. If you were lucky, they left the fringe.

Associated saying: *'Sit still or I'll cut your ear off!'* (Something you could never make out whether it was just a warning or a threat.)

5. THE 'NOW GET UP THE STAIRS AND WASH THE HAIR OUT OF YOUR HAIR' PART:

With final instructions to '*get up the stairs and wash your hair*', the ordeal ended, at least for another month. You could now relax and look forward to the prospect of being slagged in school for looking like you had recently been released from solitary confinement, unless you managed to get hold of some of your brother's hair gel the next morning.

Associated saying: '*Now get up the stairs and wash that hair out of your hair*' and/or '*feck off and buy your own hair gel!*'

THE IRISH DIASPORA

Due to periodic waves of outward migration, the population of Ireland currently living outside of Ireland is now a multiple of that living at home. This is kind of sad. Thankfully we can sometimes still incorporate these people into Irish life by allowing them access to a passport, picking them for our national football team and posting them out Denny rashers. Other times, like when it comes to voting, we can't.

While the number of our diaspora is hard to accurately define (with around 35 to 44 million Irish in the US, between 5 and 14 million in Britain and more than 4 million in Australia), below are three categories of Irish overseas, to help those abroad who feel Irish figure out where they fit in.

'REAL IRISH'

You feel Irish and ...

... were born in Ireland.

... spent your formative years in Ireland.

... have at least one Irish parent.

... have at least one Irish grandparent (who used to tell you stories or give you a sup of their port come Christmas).

'HONOURABLY IRISH'

You feel Irish and ...

... have lived at least a few years in Ireland and now use the word 'grand' and/or are unable to pronounce words with 'u' correctly (e.g. 'but', 'pub' or 'fuck').

... are going out with/married to an Irish person.

... have visited Ireland at least half a dozen times and genuinely feel that potatoes are your favourite food.

'NOT REALLY IRISH AT ALL BUT WE'LL TAKE YOU IN'

You feel Irish and ...

... talk incessantly about the weather.

... are happy when England lose at sport and enjoy watching Mel Gibson movies where he goes mad fighting for independence.

... have kissed someone with red hair.

... have rung in sick at least once after St Patrick's Day (and definitely don't refer to it as St Patty's Day).

... you are, were once or know someone who is a functioning alcoholic but still great craic.

... you sat beside someone in primary school who owned an Irish red setter.

THE LATE LATE TOY SHOW

SCHEDULE OF EVENTS:

9.27pm: 'RTÉ Weather' finishes, meaning that there are now only commercials separating a nation of children and 'The Late Late Toy Show'. A child in Clonmel throws up with the nerves.

9.30pm: 'The Toy Show' starts with the Billy Barry Kids, some of them fresh from a stint in the Betty Ford Clinic.

9.34pm: Presenter Ryan Tubridy arrives with a Christmas jumper that by rights should require a licence. Crowd cheer as they get their first free toy of the night.

9.38pm: Children travel across the stage on various forms of transport. At least one little girl freezes halfway over and has to be dragged off, while a little curly-haired blonde kid drives his electric fire-engine into the Lego display. Audience ratings can't get off to a better start.

9.43pm: Children arrive in with an array of toys. Two stand with their back to the camera. One kid, who is destined to be a dairy farmer, wins the audience over with his 'honest' assessment of a model JCB. Feminists groan as a little girl in pig-tails wheels out her 21st-century Betty Crocker kitchen set complete with toy wok. Thankfully another girl comes on with a pocket-sized science lab setting off a chemical explosion researchers didn't think was possible, burning Ryan's hand in the process. Cut to ad break.

AD BREAK

9.57pm: Ryan, dressed in a new jumper that will later cause nightmares for some viewers at home, and with a small dressing on his right hand, welcomes everyone back. Crowd cheer as they get their second toy of the night.

9.59pm: A 7-year-old plays a 17th-century symposium on the piano. A woman in Donegal cries.

10.05pm: New technology is premiered as children, who seem not very well adjusted to humans, show off their robots. By and large everyone is impressed by the toys, which have the same energy and battery needs as an emerging Chinese province.

10.18pm: A game involving some sort of weapon takes place as Ryan and a 12-year-old from Macroom do battle with the nation's current pop-stars beloved by 11–14-year-olds. Game finishes when Ryan is shot in the eye by his own team-mate.

AD BREAK

10.22pm: Ryan returns with a new jumper that is only slightly redder than his left eye. He interviews current tween heart-throbs asking them about their latest (and only) album, where they are appearing this Christmas in panto and whether they know yet if their career will last past spring.

10.33pm: Ryan gives the audience a fun family activity game set. Crowd cheer but are not satisfied.

10.35pm: Five girls and one boy go through the dolls they have been taking care of for the last week. Ryan does his best to look comfortable but the baby with the raggedy eye eventually spooks him. He finishes the segment from afar.

10.45pm: A ridiculously good teenage rock band play. They are so good that they will either split up due to artistic differences by the next ad break or become superstars.

AD BREAK

10.53pm: Ryan returns with a jumper that carries the same health warning as flash photography and introduces the reading section. The hands of children around the country take a break as they momentarily stop adding to their Santa list.

10.59pm: Ryan brings the book section to a premature end after the crowd begin to become restless and a '*give us another bleedin' toy Ryan!*' is picked up by a studio mike.

11.02pm: Producers take a gamble with an Irish toy section that seems to involve a lot of games made from wood but re-uses the cutest children from part one. Ratings soar when Ryan is hit by something from a boys-own tool kit produced in Kilkenny. If you are recording and watch his lips again very slowly, he seems to mouth a word begin with an 'F'. It doesn't appear on the Sunday edition.

11.15pm: Crap local dance group that were able to fill in on short notice, after arranged troupe came down with the winter vomiting bug, take to the floor. They bomb but viewers at home are too tired to notice while the audience in the studio are now only interested in another present. They are finally quelled by a weekend break. Some people realise this will be the last freebie and begin to leave during the final ad break.

AD BREAK

11.21pm: Computer section. Despite being what should be the most popular section in the show, RTÉ traditionalists succeed in keeping this to the end. Children who will spend their teenage years being awake well past midnight as they play online introduce the games in intricate detail. Ryan looks as exhausted as his final jumper.

11.31am: Young solo artist brings the night to a close with a beautiful version of 'Silent Night' to a half-empty studio and a satisfied nation. The woman in Donegal cries once more and Ireland now knows that Christmas is just around the corner.

HO-HO-HO

LEPRECHAUNS

A leprechaun is a type of fairy in Irish folklore who spends his time dressed in a red and green coat, making shoes and storing his gold in a large black cauldron that he hides at the end of a rainbow.

Legend has it that if you can find and capture a leprechaun, they will be forced to tell you where they kept their gold.

Nowadays we call that a 'tiger kidnapping' and thankfully due to harsher sentencing laws and the fact that the cauldrons of leprechauns are all now fitted with time delays and explosive colour dye, capturing these spirited folk has become a thing of the past. As a result they are now free to repair shoes or ask for money from visiting tourists in exchange for photographs in peace.

WiND

While it would be a stretch to say Ireland invented the wind, what we can take some pride in is that in 1805 a native of Navan, Francis Beaufort, invented the Beaufort Scale. This scale, with thirteen stages from zero to Force 12, remains the premier guide to wind conditions, as summarised and simplified below.

Beaufort number: 0
Description: Calm
Conditions: Unluckiest day in Irish Kite Flying Final history.

Beaufort number: 1
Description: Light air
Conditions: Still not a good idea to fart during a picnic.

Beaufort number: 2
Description: Light breeze
Conditions: You can smell someone having a barbecue nearby, and it's still only March!

Beaufort number: 3
Description: Gentle breeze
Conditions: Great weather for drying clothes.

Beaufort number: 4
Description: Fresh breeze
Conditions: Powerful weather for drying clothes!

Beaufort number: 5
Description: Moderate breeze
Conditions: That money you spent in the hairdresser has been wasted.

Beaufort number: 6
Description: Strong breeze
Conditions: There goes the umbrella!

Beaufort number: 7
Description: High wind, moderate gale
Conditions: Instagram almost crashes as people post photos of themselves lying into the wind.

Beaufort number: 8
Description: Fresh gale
Conditions: An old man in Tubbercurry is blown off his bike as he cycles by the gate of a field.

Beaufort number: 9

Description: Strong gale

Conditions: You'll spend the next two days looking for your wheelie bins.

Beaufort number: 10

Description: Storm

Conditions: The TV aerial is hanging on by its fingertips, slates are coming off the roof and the back-road to mass is blocked by a tree covered in ivy.

Beaufort number: 11

Description: Violent storm

Conditions: Things have gotten serious. Widespread vegetation and structural damage likely. Junior B hurling training called off.

Beaufort number: 12

Description: Hurricane force

Conditions: Apocalyptic. Gerry Fleming is brought out to present the weather, he doesn't wink good night and you realise that the howling noise that just flew past your window was Rover the dog blowing away.

IRISH BLESSINGS

While there may be few people out there that will insult, slag, sneer at, affront, abuse or offend you like the Irish, even if only in jest, it is heartening to know that at least we have some blessings too:

- ‘May the road rise to meet you.’

- ‘May the wind always be at your back.’

- ‘May the walls of your home never fall in and those within them never fall out.’

- ‘May the sun shine soft on your field.’

- ‘May the saddest day of your future be no worse than the happiest day of your past.’

- ‘May the frost never afflict your spuds.’

- ‘May the dust of your carriage blind the eyes of your foes.’

- ‘May you live for a hundred years with one extra year to repent.’

❧ *'As you slide down the banister of life, may the splinters never point in the wrong direction.'*

❧ *'May the rains sweep gentle across your fields.'*

And for when you're dead:

❧ *'May you be in heaven a half hour before the Devil knows you're gone.'*

And finally some less familiar Irish blessings that are gaining in popularity:

❧ *'May someone flash you the lights before a speed check.'*

❧ *'May you never slip on the ice and end up on YouTube.'*

❧ *'May you always meet a tractor on a straight wide road.'*

❧ *'May the collection basket skip you at mass.'*

❧ *'May your toast fall marmalade up.'*

❧ *'May your milk never leak in the back of the car.'*

❧ *'May "the bad pint" never find you.'*

THE DECEMBER 8TH SHOPPING

Every year on the short-grass plains of the Serengeti, over one million wildebeest and zebra make their annual migration, moving northwards to follow the rains. A few thousand kilometres south, hundreds of elephants brave the scorching hot weather on their journey towards the Okavango Delta along ancient annual migration trails to find solace and succour amongst its wet lands. Across the ocean in the Canadian forests, hundreds of millions of Pacific salmon return to the mountain streams in which they were born, where they will spawn and die. Such are some of nature's great annual migrations.

IN IRELAND WE CALL OURS 'THE DECEMBER 8TH SHOPPING'.

On this day every year, in rural houses across the country, lights come on before dawn as Irish mothers pack sandwiches and wake their husbands so as not to miss a good parking spot. Then when everyone is loaded they set off towards 'the Big Smoke'.

It is a journey that is fraught with danger as cars with every registration plate imaginable except 'D', make their way in across the M50 and try to successfully traverse the Red Cow roundabout and keep their nerve as they pass through Tallaght, Clondalkin and Castleknock. Many don't make it. Some lose their nerve. And others simply decide to just turn round and shop somewhere in Kildare instead. However for those who do succeed, a new world awaits of wrapping paper, Henry Street heaving, Grafton Street looking and Penneys madness.

THE SACRED VIRGIN PICTURE

In Irish kitchens there used to be seven universal ingredients:

1. Floor and ceiling

2. Wall, preferably containing window and door

3. A cooker

4. A kettle (and tea bags)

5. A fridge (or somewhere else to store the milk)

6. The presses (where the messages were stored)

7. A picture of the Sacred Heart of Jesus and/or Our Lady of Perpetual Health (aka the Virgin Mary). In certain houses a trinity was formed with the addition of a third picture, that of John F. Kennedy.

These pictures were sacrosanct. Calendars came and went, as did postcards, wedding photos and stick art from school, but pictures of Jesus and the Virgin Mary remained unmoving.

BLACK ICE

IRISH MOTORING HAZARDS COME IN THREE SHADES.

Yellow warnings:

- Funeral corteges
- A pot-hole
- Speed cameras
- Learner drivers
- Rain

Orange warnings:

- A large pot-hole
- Localised flooding
- Snow
- Fog
- Ice
- Horses loose on the M50
- Zombies

And finally ... **Red warnings:**

- Lone snipers
- Falling space debris
- Black ice

Of all these the most perilous is of course 'black ice'. Black ice is so engrained in the Irish psyche that even a whisper of it on the radio is enough to send every Irish parent to the phone ringing their children to tell them to '*be careful on the road tomorrow because they said there might be black ice*', even if that child is now living in Dubai.

IRiSH STEW

When the winter arrives and the nights close in, there is no substitute for comfort food. And while there are several comfort foods that the Irish turn to when the months start to end in '–ember', there is only one Irish stew.

Of course, while there might be just one Irish stew there seems to be no end to the types of ingredients that might go into its making: mutton, lamb, goat, beef, potatoes (of course), carrots, parsnips, turnips, parsley, pearl barley, onions, water, Guinness, pieces of old shoe, belts, handles off the drawer, etc.

The thing is, it doesn't really matter what you put in it as long as you stew it for anywhere between two hours and the latter half of November. After that, what you will be left with will be one truly tender, deliciously succulent meal that will warm the coldest of cockles.

BATTERED SAUSAGES

Battered sausages were inducted into the Irish Food Hall of Fame in 1982. Since then their legendary status has only continued to grow. While these pieces of er ... something coated in batter are amongst the most delicious reasons to eat cholesterol, there is a hidden history to battered sausages that is even more incredible than their luscious post-pint taste. For instance, most people don't know it but:

~ Two battered sausages made it onto Noah's ark.

~ A battered sausage was amongst those who left on the exodus out of Egypt.

~ There were three battered sausages along with the five loaves and two fish that helped feed the 5,000.

~ A battered sausage played backing guitar while Nero fiddled.

~ A battered sausage was amongst those who threw tea into Boston Harbour (it later refused to sign the Declaration of Independence because it didn't go far enough).

~ A battered sausage helped stem the final German counter-attack in the Ardennes.

~ A battered sausage helped carry Sherpa Tensing's gear up Mount Everest.

~ A battered sausage stayed behind with Michael Collins on Apollo 11 while Neil and Buzz went wandering outside.

~ A battered sausage helped bring down the Berlin Wall.

Of course, because it is a battered sausage, you will never read any of these. But that's the battered sausage for you: part food, part legend, part not really food.

SHOWBANDS

Brendan Bowyer and the Royals; Butch Moore and the Capitols; Eileen Reid and the Cadets; Joe Dolan and the Drifters; Big Tom and the Mainliners; Dickie Rock and the Miami Showband ...

The Eldorado; the Ierne; the Arcadia; the National; the Mecca; the Metropole; the Crystal; the Top Hat; the Olympic; the Lakeland; the Maryland; the Roseland; the Cloudland ...

Such were some of the names and places from the showband era, a time when half a generation of Ireland (the young men-folk) lined up on one side of a dance-hall and faced another half a generation (the young women-folk). Urban or rural, it didn't matter as for five shillings or so, men and women flocked to these weekend revelries to dance the night away.

It was a time when questions of '*will you dance with me?*' were sometimes met with '*no, but you can dance with my sister*'; where the pants buttons of your nearest neighbour were occasionally flicked open to give you a headstart in asking the girl of your dreams; when, if you were lucky, she would say yes and maybe even agree to come outside with you for a quick kiss, allowing you to sell your 'Pass Out' to someone looking to pass in; and when, if you were unlucky, you'd see your would-be love retreat away from you into the ladies' toilets. And throughout all this there was always the showband, going strong from 9pm until two in the morning.

It was a time of great fun and frolic – except of course during Lent.

Then, at the end of the late Cretaceous period, it suddenly died out as numbers dramatically fell away. No one really knows why but it is thought to have something to do with a sudden cooling down of the earth's atmosphere due to a meteorite hit, huge volcanic eruptions, sea-levels change and the growth of discothèque.

PREPARING FOR AN IRISH CHRISTMAS

Once the advent calendars have been opened and the annual December 8th country visit to the city for Christmas shopping has passed, the festive season in Ireland is now officially under way. In Ireland, the run up to Christmas is celebrated in its own peculiar fashion.

SOME HiGHLiGHTS:

★ The tree is bought with the annual question: shed or non-shed? To answer this, families ask that other age-old question: do you enjoy vacuuming the hell out of your carpets for pine needles from now until February or not? If the answer is no, then non-shed it is.

★ The youngest child is sent into the attic to find last year's decorations.

★ The length of an average industrial working day is lost as:

- Firstly, a location for the tree cannot be found because of the shine of the sitting room light.
- Secondly, the father spends 30 minutes trying to locate the wonky fairy-light that has gotten loose.
- Thirdly, the two youngest siblings fight it out for the right to put the little angel up on top. Throwing the 'Holy' Santa up there will eventually resolve this.

★ Someone drops a bauble and everyone is told to stop and not move an inch as the mother tiptoes out like a commando to fetch the brush and pan.

★ First finger-pointing of the festive season takes place as the little baby Jesus from crib cannot be found. A small Chocolate Eclair from the selection box is used as a temporary measure.

★ One member of the family (usually a daughter who is vegetarian) suggests buying something other than a turkey. Announcing she was pregnant and has narrowed the possible fathers down to four would get a more favourable response.

★ While siblings were once given £5 and a half hour to scurry round Henry Street and buy tat for the family, nowadays the 'Kris Kringle' reigns supreme. In Ireland this sees family members secretly pick out a member of the clan to buy one large gift for. They will then secretly swap the names they have picked with each other and then secretly ask their 'pick' what they want.

★ 31 tins of biscuits and sweets are bought. These will make up the annual biscuit tin merry-go-round as aunts and uncles spend the pre-Christmas period driving round to each other swapping tins. This will inevitably mean that you will end up with exactly 31 biscuit and sweet tins that will last until June.

★ Word goes round the siblings that a bag of Brussels sprouts was spotted in the local supermarket. Panic sets in.

★ Father contravenes several health and safety regulations as he attempts to wire the lights out front.

★ Youngest child is used again, this time to run out of the car on a drive-by to rob holly from a house up the road.

★ Mother retreats into the front room for two days to write Christmas cards to extended family members who only exist at Christmas.

★ A new baby Jesus is bought to replace the Chocolate Eclair. It is unclear where it comes from but it is definitely not the son of Mary.

COMING HOME FOR CHRISTMAS

Ireland, the night before: Your sister rings you to check for the umpteenth time to see if you are still planning to collect the brother from the airport tomorrow. Because if you're not, she is happily prepared to take her little ones and make the 100-mile round journey to meet him. You know she's serious.

Meanwhile many, many miles away: Your brother transits sleepily through New York, Abu Dhabi or Dubai waiting for the last leg home. If he's closer to home, already in, say, London, he decides to pack the rest of his clothes in the morning. The presents are in, that's all that matters.

10.36am: '*Where are ya?*' your father asks you. '*I'm on the road just passing Kiltale*', you lie. (You've only just left Trim but there's no point worrying him. It's the weekend. There is no traffic heading towards Dublin. The roads are dry and you'll be at the airport before the brother even lands.)

Meanwhile: Despite being only 40 minutes to landing, your brother begins his second movie of the morning. He decides he can always watch the rest on video. Immigration cards are being offered but the stewards are lucky if more than a handful is given out. All those aboard are Irish. Below him the United Kingdom looks sunny and green.

11.19am: You make such great time that you station yourself along with the anoraks up the slip-road watching 737s and Airbuses come in to land. You're only waiting for the one that's due in at 11.23.

Meanwhile: For once the clouds don't come out to greet your brother and he can see Dublin Bay crawl out towards Lambay Island; Bray Head in the distance; the Pigeon Stacks and Howth over to his right. The plane is giddy with excitement; most are smiling and he can even spot a few tears if he looks hard enough as young parents tell their young children that this is where they also call home.

11.22am: You recognise the livery and realise that this is it, Emirate EK 161. Like you heard someone once say, you can hardly believe the plane comes so low in to land! You wave as it brakes going past you, still topping 100 km/h and then you jump back into the car to find parking and a place at arrivals.

Meanwhile: Passengers can barely stop themselves from opening the luggage bins as the plane hits the tarmac. Only the most patient and understanding of stewards can stop them. Half the plane can't believe it's not raining, half the rest can't believe they're home. Your brother waits for his foreign phone to pick up signal. It does and he texts '*I'm back*'.

11.32am: You arrive at arrivals and with a hundred others you wait. The doors ahead of you slide open to reveal uncles, aunts, fathers, mothers, sons, daughters, sisters, friends. A pair of 5-year-olds make a break for it as their Dad, who's been working out on the Pilbara, comes into view. They knock his phone right out of his hand as they jump into him. Even the taxi drivers with their signs out smile at that one and then well up as the kid's mother can't help herself and runs over too and they all crumple into each other. After a minute of mutual tears, the father returns to pick up his phone and the crowd go back to looking for their loved ones.

Meanwhile: Dublin's immigration staff work their hardest as they shift from one elbow to another double-quick time waving the homecomers home, '*Grand, grand, grand, grand ...*' In the queue, your brother debates if he really needs to wait for his bag at the carousel as his presents are in his carry-on and he probably still has enough underwear in the family house to get him through to Wednesday. He decides since he's spent the best part of a day travelling, he can wait a minute more.

11.38am: You think about asking someone what flight they were on as another bundle of passengers exits and still no sign of the brother but just as you are about to approach someone whose bag clearly says Dubai Duty Free …

Meanwhile: Your brother's bag actually comes out early and he is gone! He heads for the customs channels and goes for the blue, nothing to declare. After all he only has presents and he hasn't been near a farm. He's been over-seas working, but now he's home. The doors slide open and …

11.39am: Two brothers meet.

BiSCUiT TiNS (ESPECiALLY THOSE WiTH THE PiNK WAFER BiSCUiTS)

THERE ARE TEN RULES OF BiSCUiT TiNS:

1. The first rule of biscuit tins is that you do not go down to the bottom layer of biscuit tins until the mother says it's okay to do so.

2. The second rule of biscuit tins is that you do not go down to the bottom layer of biscuit tins until the mother says it's okay to do so.

3. The third rule of biscuit tins is that you can't take more than more than two biscuits at a time and no two should be of the same of biscuit.

4. The fourth rule of biscuit tins is that the pink wafer ones hold special status. This is partly due to the

fact that they used to be used as a form of currency and party because a hundred years ago people gave up their lives so that we can have the pink wafer ones. (Or was that for freedom?)

5. The fifth rule of biscuit tins is never, ever leave the lid open.

6. The sixth rule of biscuit tins is that the mother always has first dibs on the ones with jam in them.

7. The seventh rule of biscuit tins is that in the same way certain families are divided by civil war politics, families are also divided between those that like bourbon creams and those that don't.

8. The eighth rule of biscuit tins is that there is always one biscuit that no one really likes, no matter what county you're from. (We're looking at you, only-good-for-dipping-in-tea biscuit.) It is only in the box due to some sort of 'affirmative action' for biscuits and everyone should take a turn eating at least one.

9. The ninth rule of biscuit tins is never before dinner or there will be absolutely no jelly and ice-cream for you!

10. The tenth and final rule of biscuit tins is that you will be sick of them by St Stephen's Day.

AN IRISH CHRISTMAS

THE DEFINITIVE TIMETABLE
OF AN IRISH CHRISTMAS:

EARLY, EARLY MORNING

5.32am: First child in the house wakes up (ergo everyone wakes up) and finds out what Santa brought them. Santa wishes they had gotten more sleep and finds out very quickly what toys he or she forgot to get batteries for.

MORNING

9.03am: Like a Fleetwood Mac/Rolling Stones/Eagles reunion, the family, in their most colourful new jumpers, arrive at church for their annual '*we're all back together*' tour.

9.53am: Mother cooks jumbo breakfast, as if she didn't have enough work to do.

11.05am: Christmas turkey enters its 14th hour of cooking.

12.00pm: The house is hushed as the Pope appears on television. It's hard to understand what he is saying but you guess it's something that involves blessing the Christian family and being careful not to eat too much stuffing.

12.10pm: Traditional family run, walk or jump into water so cold that you won't feel your toes again until the Brussels sprouts.

12.53pm: *It's a Wonderful Life/Charlie and the Chocolate Family/The Snowman* concludes with at least one member of the family saying '*I can't believe I've never watched that before*' and another going '*thank feck that's over for another year!*'

EARLY AFTERNOON

1.41pm: Child who is destined to get the most marks in their Leaving Cert sets the table as those who will be lucky to get a PLC course continue playing on the computer.

1.50pm: Father arrives to cut the turkey. It doesn't matter if one of the sons has since grown up to be a tree surgeon – the kitchen knife is too dangerous for everyone except the father.

2.00pm: Family begin their Christmas dinner.

2.12pm: Mother sits down and begins her Christmas dinner.

3.00pm: The Queen's speech. The cutlery is put down as around the country, families listen closely to hear what her Royal Majesty will say about ... Do they feck!

No, instead it's cracker time as the worst jokes all year are told. The prizes inside are as usual a bit of a let-down with the red fish that curls up in your palm if you are destined to find love this year or win a car in a raffle the annual highlight.

3.14pm: Dinner officially comes to an end once the first paper hat rips off on its own accord.

AFTERNOON

3.27pm: Family presents are shared. Something goes horribly wrong and Dad ends up with the foot-spa, Mam gets a jumper, Timmy (aged 8) the kitchen set, Mary (aged 6) the fire-engine, wee Emma (aged 3) gets an anthology of Russian short stories while Nana (aged 68) ends up with *Grand Theft Auto VII*.

3.43pm: Great Christmas clear up as the whole family pretends they need to sleep off the turkey and ham, leaving it to the kid who is going to get 580 points in her Leaving Cert to help with the washing.

4.00pm: Indiana Jones, Marty McFly or Luke Skywalker joins the fray.

4.40pm: Mandatory hour break from food (sometimes called 'the surface interval of the Irish digestive tract') concludes and the mother breaks out the dessert!

4.57pm: Extended family time as: either cousins call up (with better presents than you) or you ring your cousins overseas (who have presents you've never heard of).

EVENING

5.57pm: Some bastard has been putting the wrappers back into the selection box, broken through unannounced to the second layer of biscuits and eaten all the pink wafer ones! A cousin is blamed to avoid further dispute (despite only speaking to them over the internet).

7.00pm: The 'Coronation Street'/'EastEnders'/'Fair City' Christmas Special cock-blocks the action adventure recent release that RTÉ paid big bucks to show this year meaning the older kids will have to ... read! Selection boxes bear the brunt of their anger.

NiGHT

8.10pm: Last bit of motherly strength goes into making turkey sandwiches and tea.

8.48pm: Place seems strangely quiet until someone figures out the children haven't been seen since sun-down. They are found huddled together in a state of total exhaustion around a sea of toys. They are put to bed and the remaining alcohol is opened.

9.56pm: Annual family board game begins and you wonder a) how it is possible for your sister to be physiologically unable to draw anything at Pictionary without first drawing a circle, even if what she is being asked the draw is a square and b) why your Dad never gets any better at charades despite playing it for the last 24 years.

11.20pm: Tempers begin to fray after someone skips your go, throws the dice twice or sinks your battleship.

11.55pm: Eldest son manages to eat the 250th Quality Street/Rose/Celebration and the hot whiskeys finally run out, thus announcing the end to the day's proceedings.

ST STEPHEN'S DAY

THE ODDS:

8/1: That you will be nursing a hangover until noon

1/10: That you will be eating turkey and ham for dinner

6/4: That the sequel to yesterday's big family movie will be on TV

5/2: That watching sport will form some part of your day

15/2: That gambling on sport will form some part of your day

9/1: That watching sport you've gambled on will form part of your day

500/1: That someone on BBC News will refer to the day as St Stephen's Day and not Boxing Day

4/1: That the Wren Boys (also known as Straw Boys or Mummers) will scare the bejaysus out of any child under the age of 8 when they come calling to your door

20/1: That someone genuinely knows where the Wren Boys came from

5/6: That you will be sick of biscuits from the tin at this stage

Evens: That you will be wearing something you got as a present yesterday

150/1: That there will still be a seat free at the bar in your local by 9.00pm

NOT BEING ABLE TO COPE WITH WINTER

In Ireland, along with our different styles, types and varieties of weather, we also have three distinct categories.

1. The temperature band between 3°C and 20°C that we have for about 95% of the year, which includes those occasional nightfall dips below zero. This is the bread-and-butter category of weather that forms the foundation of every daily conversation.

2. The +20°C (+ 68°F) category of weather that makes up about 4% of the year and can happen any time from March to the Indian summer in early October. It is also known as the *'isn't Ireland the greatest place to live in earth in this type of weather, if only it lasted more than eight days a year'* category.

3. This category comes perhaps once a year, 1% of the time, generally either in December or January. This is when the weather never gets above 2°C (36°F) during the day and freezes its pants off at night at between -2° and -10° (14–28°F). While countries at our degree of latitude would lap this up, in Ireland we call this the '*not being able to cope with winter*' category of weather!

At this time, the schools close; we run out of grit; we curse the day we ever wanted a white Christmas; we have no clothes that can actually keep us warm outside and curse ourselves for not buying the Alpine jackets Lidl were selling for €20 last July; the radiators are on full blast and there is a blow-heater in the attic to keep the pipes from freezing; household panic sets in South County Dublin and middle-income earners start running water to stop the taps from going; low-cholesterol table salt undergoes a compulsory purchase order; RTÉ news has an item about a farmer in East Galway having to row a boat to get hay to his sheep, which plays on repeat; even black ice won't stray outside; and a man in Dublin falls over and bangs his head.

HOT WHISKEY

INGREDIENTS:

- Whiskey
- Lemon
- Cloves
- Sugar (honey)

WHAT ELSE YOU WILL NEED:

- A kettle on the boil
- A warm glass with a spoon inside to prevent it from cracking
- Weather outside cold enough to freeze the *liathróidí* off a brass monkey
- The door shut
- High stools at the bar or the bed within sight
- The flu (optional)

SERVING SUGGESTION:

- Lots of it
- Poured regularly into a glass

THE HOLY DiP

Like a miniature version of the holy water font as you enter or exit mass, the Holy Dip is the Irish household's answer to rubbing a lucky rabbit's foot on the way out of the home.

The Holy Dip has the capacity to guarantee the safety of 'the dipper' for the entire duration of their time outside their home. Positioned near the light switch inside the front door, only turning off the immersion is more important than getting a Holy Dip on the way out the house, something that you are reminded of daily by your mother:

> *'Are you off to the shop? Make sure you get yourself a dip on the way out.'*

> *'Are you off to your friend's next door? Make sure you get yourself a dip on the way out.'*

> *'Are you off down the shops? Make sure you get yourself a dip on the way out.'*

> *'Are you off to the pub? Make sure you get yourself a dip on the way out.'*

> *'Are you off fishing along the continental shelf of Alaska? Make sure you get yourself a dip on the way out.'*

> *'Are you off to war? Make sure you get yourself a dip on the way out.'*

Finally, the Holy Dip also comes in a small travel-companion-sized bottle. This allows mothers to pack it discretely into your rucksack, something you often only discover when US customs start asking questions about it.

THE END